About the Au

Photo of Patti and Tom Mount in Grand Cayman. Photo by Jim Kozmik.

Tom Mount, D.Sc. - Tom is the CEO of IANTD. He holds a MS in health sciences, a D.Sc in martial sciences and is completing a Ph.D/ND program in Naturopathic Medicine, plus a Th.D with emphasis in Intuitive Medicine. Tom is a diving pioneer from the early cave diving days, through the introduction of deep diving and mixed gas diving to the recreational market (technical diving), continuing on to formulation of original concepts accepted in CCR diving today. He received the NOGI award for sports education, Beneath the Sea's Diver of The Year award, and numerous other recognitions from various diving associations and NOAA. He is the author of numerous IANTD textbooks such as Cave Diving, Advanced Deeper Diving, and CCR Normoxic Trimix manuals. Other works include; Safe Cave Diving, Practical Diving, The New Practical Diving, Mixed Gas Diving, Technical Diver Encyclopedia, and The Greatest Adventure - Photography. Additionally, he has published over 400 articles and technical papers on all aspects of diving. Tom is also a highly accomplished Martial artist and two-time inductee to the United States Martial Arts Hall of Fame. He is the SOKE and 10th Dan in Ki Survival Systems, 9th Dan in Kick Boxing, 8th Dan in Taekwon Do, 7th Dan in Hapkido, Dim Mak Instructor, Qi Gong Instructor, 4th Dan in Judo, and 2nd Dan in Karate (1966).

David Doolette, Ph.D. - David is a research Fellow in the Department of Anesthesia and Intensive Care, University of Adelaide/Royal Adelaide Hospital, Australia. Trained in neurophysiology and nueropharmacology, he is also interested in diving physiology. His current research areas include: function of the nervous system; decompression procedures, decompression illness and health management in occupational divers; and basic mechanisms of inert gas exchange. He is an adviser for diving physiology to the recreational and occupational diving industry in Australia. David has been diving since 1979 and is now primarily involved with underwater cave exploration in Australia. In addition to exploration, he has been responsible for design of decompression protocols, design of mixed gas diving procedures and health management for extended duration caving.

David Sawatzky, M.D. - David is a Diving Medical Specialist on contract with Defence Research and Development Toronto (formerly DCIEM) since 1998. He was previously with the Canadian Forces as the Staff Officer in Hyperbaric Medicine at DCIEM and later as the Senior Medical Officer at Garrison Support Unit Toronto. He writes a monthly column for Diver Magazine, is on the Board of Advisors for the International Association of Nitrox and Technical Divers (IANTD), and is an active cave, trimix, and closed circuit diver/instructor. David still spends as much time diving as possible, but admits that at the moment his #1 awesome infant son, Lukas, is a higher priority than diving.

Lee Somers, Ph.D. - Lee has authored numerous texts and articles on diving, including the *Advanced Nitrox Diver Manual and Workbook* for IANTD, and he also contributed to the IANTD *Technical Diver Encyclopedia*. Lee was formerly the Scientific Diving Officer at the University of Michigan, and he is an extremely experienced technical and saturation diver. Before retiring, Lee held leadership positions with a variety of organizations within the diving industry, including NAUI and the YMCA.

Table of Contents

Chapter 1 - Dive Planning   5
by Tom Mount, D.Sc. and Lee Somers, Ph.D.

Chapter 2 - Equipment   16
by Tom Mount, D.Sc.

Chapter 3 - Oxygen   30
by David Sawatzky, M.D.

Chapter 4 - Narcosis   35
by David Doulette, Ph.D.

Chapter 5 - Decompression Sickness   43
by David Sawatzky, M.D.

Chapter 6 - Diving & Psychology   50
by Tom Mount, D.Sc.

Chapter 7 - Dive Technique   65
by Tom Mount, D.Sc.

Future Training Tracks   68

Glossary of Terms   69

References & Cited Works   71

The deep diver has some very important dive planning considerations. The aspects of dive planning from previous courses must be included, plus additional gas management and gas mixture issues. The complete dive plan will include the concepts you have previously been introduced to such as; site information, buddy selection and responsibilities, environmental assessment and type of dive platform. These basic dive-planning issues should be ingrained into you by now, and this chapter will address new elements that the deeper diver must include. A dive planning form will guide you through the above steps. Refer to the form that is included in this chapter.

Oxygen Management

A deep diver must carefully plan out the gas mixtures for oxygen content to ensure they remain within the oxygen tolerance zones and that the bottom time and decompression requirements may be optimized. Factors that effect the oxygen planning include dive duration, depth and decompression needs. As a Tek Lite diver, whether you are becoming an Advanced Nitrox Diver or an Advanced Recreational Trimix Diver, you will be allowed to use EAN 50 for decompression with total decompression stop times up to 15 minutes. When the bottom time and decompression times are totaled the diver must remain within safe oxygen limits, which requires careful planning. In this course the diver will be limited to a maximum partial pressure of 1.6 ATA for any phases of the dive and reduced partial pressures if the dive is within 80% of the oxygen exposure limits. For all practical purposes the bottom mix will not exceed a PO_2 of 1.5. In addition if the diver anticipates a strenuous or exceptionally cold dive, modifications must be made. As a result many divers limit the maximum partial pressure of oxygen to 1.4 ATA for the target operating depth (TOD), which is the planned operational depth and 1.6 ATA for the maximum operating depth (MOD). In this case, that would be the maximum obtainable depth or a "what if" depth on the dive. When planning dives the oxygen exposure and decompression requirements will dictate the safe duration of a dive.

Take oxygen seriously! Plan to stay within the recommended limits for both central nervous system (CNS) and pulmonary toxicity. According to the CNS/OTU table in this text, you will find that 1.5 ATA gives a diver 120 minutes of oxygen exposure time.

Planning for the Best Mix & MOD

You can now calculate the "best mix" for a given set of diving conditions based on the PO_2 you have chosen. Let's assume that you wish to dive to a depth of 140 fsw (42 msw). The planned dive incorporates moderate water temperatures and exertion due to current. For this reason the dive is planned with a maximum PO_2 of 1.45 ATA.

$$FO_{2(maximum)} = \frac{PO_{2(maximum)}}{\left(\frac{D_{(fsw)}}{33} + 1\right)} \quad or \quad FO_{2(maximum)} = \frac{PO_{2(maximum)}}{\left(\frac{D_{(msw)}}{10} + 1\right)}$$

Substituting oxygen and depth values:

$$FO_{2(maximum)} = \frac{1.45ATA}{\left(\frac{142_{(fsw)}}{33} + 1\right)} \quad or \quad FO_{2(maximum)} = \frac{1.45 ATA}{\left(\frac{42_{(msw)}}{10} + 1\right)}$$

From the above the maximum FO_2 for this dive is 27.67 % (round off to 28%).

Maximum Operating Depth

You can calculate the maximum operating depth (MOD) in feet or meters of seawater for any selected PO_2 using the formula:

$$MOD_{(fsw)} = \left[\left(\frac{P_g}{F_g}\right) - 1\right] 33 \quad or \quad MOD_{(msw)} = \left[\left(\frac{P_g}{F_g}\right) - 1\right] 10$$

Where **Pg** is the desired partial pressure of oxygen and **Fg** is the fraction of oxygen in the gas mixture. For example, you can also determine the target operating depth (TOD) for breathing EAN 36 without exceeding a PO_2 of 1.5 ATA as follows:

$$TOD_{(fsw)} = \left[\left(\frac{1.5}{0.36}\right) - 1\right] 33 \quad or \quad TOD_{(msw)} = \left[\left(\frac{1.5}{0.36}\right) - 1\right] 10$$

TOD = 104.5 fsw   or   TOD = 31.7 msw.

The MOD in this case is solved using the same equation, except with a PO_2 of 1.6 ATA or 113.6 fsw (34.4 msw). In the event of a strenuous or a cold-water dive the TOD will be planned at a PO_2 of 1.4 ATA.

Equivalent Air Depth

At the dive site you analyze your gas and discover the mixture contains 32% oxygen. If the planned dive is to 100 fsw (30 msw), what is the equivalent air depth (EAD) depth?

$$EAD_{(fsw)} = \left[\frac{(FN_2)(D+33)}{0.79}\right] - 33 \quad \text{or} \quad EAD_{(msw)} = \left[\frac{(FN_2)(D+10)}{0.79}\right] - 10$$

Where FN_2 is the decimal fraction of nitrogen in the mixture and D is the depth in feet or meters, assume that your analysis reveals that the mixture contains only 32% oxygen and you are planning to dive to a MOD of 100 fsw (30.5 msw). Is this mix appropriate for this depth? You can quickly calculate MOD using the above formula. Entering the value of .32 for the fraction of oxygen:

$$MOD = \left[\left(\frac{1.6}{0.32}\right) - 1\right]33 \quad \text{or} \quad MOD = \left[\left(\frac{1.6}{0.32}\right) - 1\right]10$$

The MOD for this mixture is 99 fsw (30.2 msw). In theory, you would only have to adjust your maximum depth limit by 1 fsw (0.3 msw). Always maintain a reasonable and conservative depth and oxygen limit.

The maximum depths for various oxygen percentages based on desired oxygen partial pressure are given in the IANTD EAD/MOD Table.

You can now substitute the new values for depth and nitrogen fraction into the *EAD* formula:

$$EAD = \left[\frac{(.68)(100+33)}{0.79}\right] - 33 \quad \text{or} \quad EAD(msw) = \left[\frac{(.68)(30+10)}{0.79}\right] - 10$$

To find that the equivalent air depth is fsw (msw), use your fsw (msw) schedule on your air table. If the diver were using trimix 32/15 (32% Oxygen and 15% Helium) instead of EAN 32, the EAD would be shallower as determined below.

$$EAD = \left[\frac{(.53)(100+33)}{0.79}\right] - 33 \quad \text{or} \quad EAD(msw) = \left[\frac{(.53)(30+10)}{0.79}\right] - 10$$

The above mixture is referred to as trimix 32/15 and the addition of 15% helium dropped the EAD to 56 fsw (16.8 msw). The reduced narcosis exposure is obvious with the introduction of helium to the mixture. As an added example let's look at a dive to 140 fsw (42 msw) using trimix 28/25:

In this case the mixture of 28/25 would provide

$$EAD = \left[\frac{(.53)(140+33)}{0.79}\right] - 33 \quad \text{or} \quad EAD(msw) = \left[\frac{(.53)(42+10)}{0.79}\right] - 10$$

an EAD (or narcosis level) of 83 fsw or (24.8 msw), had this same dive been on EAN 28 the narcosis level would have been 124.6 fsw or (37.39 msw).

$$EAD = \left[\frac{(.72)(140+33)}{0.79}\right] - 33 \quad \text{or} \quad EAD(msw) = \left[\frac{(.72)(42+10)}{0.79}\right] - 10$$

The comparison between trimix 28/25 and EAN 28 illustrates the advantage of trimix versus nitrox mixtures for reducing narcosis on dives.

Tracking Oxygen Exposure

When planning the dive, it is important to track oxygen exposure. Track the neurological (CNS) risks and the total body risks of oxygen exposure.

The CNS risks may be determined by dividing the actual exposure time at a given partial pressure of oxygen by the allotted time for that exposure. However, an easier and more effective way to plan oxygen exposures is using the IANTD EAD/MOD table.

When using this table find the selected PO_2 - these begin at EAN 24 and go up to 100% oxygen. The mix is on the far left as you face the table. Follow across and see different depths below (this one will see the EAD), continuing downward the PO_2 is shown, below that the OTUs per minute, and last the CNS exposure. The far right column lists the MOD at various PO_2 levels.

This chart is a valuable dive-planning tool. A waterproof version is included with the Advanced EANx and Advanced Recreational Trimix student kits. This table helps you complete an entire gas plan using EANx.

Notes:

MOD
max operating depth $PO_2 = 1.4 \, 1.6$

F fraction of gas

- & how do these go as compared to PADI EANx?

BEST MIX

$FO_2 = PO_2 \div ATA \, (depth)$

$FN_2 = \dfrac{ATA}{END} \times 0.79$ over $ATA \, (depth)$

$FHe = 1.00 - FO_2 - FN_2$

eg. 45 mtrs:

$FO_2 = 1.5 / 5.5 = 27\%$

$FN_2 = \dfrac{3.4 \times 0.79}{5.5} = 49\%$

$FHe = 1 - 0.27 - 0.49 =$

27/24

Another useful dive planning tool is the IANTD OTU/CNS Tracking Table that is also included in your student kit. When using this table go to the PO_2 and the dive time at that PO_2 which ranges from 1 to 60 minutes. Included, are a PO_2 and CNS repetitive dive planner tables.

For Advanced Recreational Trimix computations of EAD/END refer to:

ACTUAL DEPTH	EQUIVALENT NARCOSIS DEPTHS						
		END 60 FSW 18 MSW		END 70 FSW 21 MSW		END 80 FSW 24 MSW	
FSW/MSW	Fi O2	Fi HE	Fi N2	Fi HE	Fi N2	Fi HE	FI N2
90 / 27	0.38	0.00	n/a	n/a	n/a	n/a	n/a
100 / 30	0.34	0.11	0.55	0.05	0.61	0.00	0.67
110 / 33	0.32	0.17	0.51	0.11	0.57	0.06	0.62
120 / 36	0.30	0.22	0.48	0.17	0.53	0.12	0.58
130 / 39	0.28	0.27	0.45	0.22	0.50	0.17	0.55
140 / 42	0.27	0.30	0.43	0.26	0.47	0.21	0.52
150 / 45	0.26	0.34	0.40	0.29	0.45	0.25	0.49

When diving the 32/15 IANTD trimix table, the nitrogen content in the tables is 53%. The table below provides the END from 90-130 ft for this mix.

Trimix 32/15

DEPTH		END (rounded to nearest depth)	
fsw	msw	fsw	msw
90	27	49	15
100	30	56	17
110	33	63	19
120	36	70	21
130	39	76	23

If one uses the IANTD 28/25 trimix tables the fraction of nitrogen in the mixture will be 0.47.

Trimix 28/25

DEPTH		END (rounded to nearest depth)	
fsw	msw	fsw	msw
100	30	46	14
110	33	52	16
120	36	58	17
130	39	64	19
140	42	70	21
150	45	76	23

Inert Gas Management

In Advanced EANx or Advanced Recreational Trimix diver training you will learn to use the IANTD EANx and or Recreational Trimix Dive Tables. The EANx tables were derived from the Buhlmann Swiss Air Tables (ZH-L$_{16}$ system) using the equivalent air depth technique. The Buhlmann tables are among the most widely used dive tables in the world. The ZH-L$_{16}$ system is used to calculate both staged and continuous decompression and is programmed into many current dive computers. The tables for Recreational Trimix diving were produced based on the Variable Permeable Membrane (VPM) model. The VPM tables utilized deeper stops and thus were considered more appropriate for use with Helium based mixtures for this course.

IANTD Dive Tables: Definitions

Depths listed are the maximum depths reached during a dive.

Bottom Time is the time from leaving the surface until commencing final ascent to the surface or any decompression stop(s).

Decompression Stop Time is the time actually spent at that stop. It does not include the time required to ascend to the stop.

Repetitive Group is a measure of excess nitrogen remaining in the body after a dive.

Surface Interval is the time from surfacing from a dive to commencing the next descent.

Residual Nitrogen Time is a measure of the amount of excess nitrogen still in the body at the end of the surface interval. It is the time that the diver must consider that he has already spent at the planned depth of the repetitive dive when commencing a repetitive dive.

IANTD EANx Dive Tables: Rules
Ascent rate must not exceed 33 ft/min (10 m/min)

1. Use exact or next greater dive depth and time for entering the table. (Example: For a dive to 44 fsw (13.5 msw) for 26 minutes breathing EAN 32, use the

50 fsw (15 msw) schedule for 30 minutes.

2. Repetitive dives require additional time to be added. The time is determined by using the repetitive dive table and is called the Residual Nitrogen Time (RNT). The RNT is a measure of any excess nitrogen already in the diver's body before a repetitive dive.

3. If the depth of the repetitive dive is between two increments, use the *shallower* figure when calculating residual nitrogen time (this gives a greater RNT and is thus safer).

4. A safety stop of three to five minutes at 15 fsw (4.5 msw) is required during ascent from any no-decompression stop dive (up to an altitude of 1000 ft or 300 m).

IANTD EANx Tables: General Instructions

1. Enter Section A at the row corresponding to maximum dive depth fsw/msw, and then look downward until the diver bottom time is found (Section B). The exact or next greater rule applies for interim depths and times. Follow across to the right to read the repetitive group letter. Repetitive group letters are also provided for decompression dives on the back of the table.

2. Enter Section C horizontally (across) to find the appropriate Surface Interval Time (SIT).

3. Read the new repetitive group designation letter (Section D) in the same column below.

4. For subsequent dives, read the residual nitrogen time (RNT) from Section E at the intersection of the column containing the repetitive group designation letter and row containing the maximum depth of the subsequent dive. For intermediate depths use the next **shallower** depth.

5. Add the residual nitrogen time (RNT) to the diver's actual bottom time (ABT) to determine total bottom time (TBT). Total bottom time is used in subsequent calculations for decompression, repetitive group, etc.

6. If Nitrox containing 50% oxygen is used during decompression, the corresponding decompression time can be found on the reverse side of the table.

7. IANTD encourages divers to remain at surface

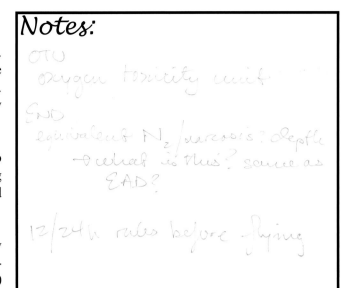

Notes:

OTU
oxygen toxicity unit

END
equivalent N₂/narcosis? depth
→ what is this? same as
EAD?

12/24h rules before flying

pressure for a minimum of 12 hours, longer is preferable, following no-decompression dives. And, at least 24 hours following decompression dives before ascending to altitude up to 8,000 ft cabin pressure in a commercial airliner.

Now let's plan a three dive series using the Nitrogen Management Chart and IANTD EANx Tables that were included with your student kit.

Using Dive Computers

Nitrox dive computers are commonplace in today's industry. Recently several manufacturers have introduced models with Helium based mixtures and some include constant partial pressure programs. These computers allow the dive gas to be programmed. Most of the more advanced dive computers allow for gas changes during the dive. Therefore, the computer can be used for all diving needs. Depending on the model, they may be programmed manually or by interfacing with your personal computer. Modern computer programs are easy to use and facilitate detailed dive planning as well as dive documentation. Some mixed gas dive computers are gas-supply integrated to provide information on cylinder pressure and gas use status; others are independently attached to the diver.

A complete discussion of dive computers is beyond the scope of this manual since each model of dive computer requires specific procedures instructions and procedures for use. Only a generalized overview is presented here. Users must read and understand the manufacturer's instruction manual that is supplied with each computer.

What is a Dive Computer?

This general discussion of dive computers was adapted by the author from a paper titled, *"Dive Computers: Uses and Abuses"* by Karl Huggins.

A dive computer (DC) is just that, a computer. It does not, as some people think, monitor the amount of nitrogen in a diver's body. All it does is compute decompression status according to a mathematical model. It senses depth and time during the dive and then the decompression status is read or computed based on a mathematical model. This decompression status information is displayed to the diver, who uses it as an additional source of information for diving.

Dive Computers: General Component Definitions

Pressure Transducer that converts the ambient pressure surrounding the diver to a signal that is fed into the input of the A/D Converter (see definition below).

A/D (Analog to Digital) Converter that changes the pressure transducer signal to a digital "word" that can be "read" by the microprocessor.

Microprocessor the "brain" that controls the signal flows and performs the mathematical and logical operations.

ROM (Read Only Memory) a non-volatile memory that contains the program steps, which "tell" the microprocessor what to do. The ROM also contains the constants used in the mathematical model that determines the diver's decompression status.

RAM (Random Access Memory) contains the storage registers in which variable data and results are stored during computations.

Display that presents the diver's decompression status.

Clock that synchronizes the operational steps of the microprocessor and is used as the time input.

Power Supply that runs the device.

Device Housing that protects the components from the environment.

The algorithms used in dive computers are mathematical and logical formulas with variables of depth and time, which makes them much more flexible than tables. A pure mathematical model affords an infinite number of depth and time solutions. Dive tables are finite listings of some of the solutions produced from a mathematical model.

Tables base decompression status on the assumption that the entire dive was spent at the maximum depth. Most scuba divers spend only a small fraction of their dive time at the deepest depth achieved during the dive. This means that during most of the dive the diver is taking on less nitrogen than assumed by the tables.

Model based dive computers that update the diver's status every few seconds will compensate for the changes in depth. This allows the diver to be presented with a decompression status based on the actual dive that was performed. The advantages of computing decompression status in this manner include:

1. Profile Integration (no maximum depth entire dive assumption).
2. Shallow portions of dive (safety stops) are taken into account.
3. Actual Depth used in Calculation (51 fsw/15.5 msw, not 60 fsw/18.3 msw).
4. All compartments of the model are taken into account when calculating multi-level dive profiles (most table based techniques utilize the compartment representing their repetitive groups).

However, many of the advantages of dive computers can ultimately become disadvantages. If the device is pushed to its limit, the model is too. A diver needs to read the device, understand the information presented and act upon that information. The major disadvantage, shared by tables and dive computers alike, is all the computer or table knows about is depth and time.

Decompression models do not actually represent what is happening in the body. All models attempt to produce depth-time combinations that are safe for most divers, most of the time. Nearly all decompression models to date use the two variables, depth and time. These are used to compute the decompression status displayed to the diver. Many other factors can change the diver's susceptibility to decompression sickness. These include ascent rate, physical exertion, water temperature, physical condition, hydration and blood-alcohol level, age, gender, breathing mixture, etc.

If two divers perform the same depth-time dive profile, one being low exertion by a young healthy diver in a warm Caribbean environment and the other, performed under high exertion in cold water by an older, out-of-shape, hung-over diver then the same decompression status will be computed by a dive computer (if the same model is used). However, today some dive computers may be user-programmed with a conservatism factor.

Divers must be aware that they need to add safety factors based on their own physiological state, the diving environment, and their previous dive profiles, just as they have been taught to do when using tables.

Divers must realize that they need to take responsibility for their actions and safety. They must acknowledge the fact that every time they dive, there are

risks involved. One of these risks is the possibility of developing decompression sickness. A diver needs to make a risk-benefit assessment as part of the dive plan. The goal of such an assessment is to maximize the benefit while minimizing the risk.

The operation and limitation(s) of the dive

> **"Divers must be aware that they need to add safety factors based on their own physiological state, the diving environment, and their previous dive profiles, just as they have been taught to do when using tables."**

computers being used need to be understood. The more the diver understands about the equipment being used, the more educated and safe the decisions will become.

Dive computers should not be pushed to their limits. Divers should add safety factors just as they are added with table use. Remember, all a dive computer knows about is depth and time. Dive computers are not anti-decompression sickness talismans. They will not ward off bubble formation or suck the nitrogen from the body. Most of all, a diver needs to employ common sense in all phases of diving.

Some important things to keep in mind when using a dive computer:

• Completely read the manufacturer's manual and instructions for using the dive computer and follow recommended guidelines. If you do not understand the instructions, consult an instructor or the manufacturer for clarification.

• A single computer should not be shared between divers. If participating in computer-assisted diving, each diver should use an individual computer. Many divers also carry a second or backup computer.

- Make the deepest portion of your dive first and work progressively shallower throughout the dive.

- Always follow the more conservative computer within the buddy team.

- If your computer fails, make a normal ascent (if you have remained within the no-decompression limits) and stop at 15 fsw (3 msw) for at least 5 minutes. The manufacturer's manual for your computer will provide instructions relative to how long you must stay out of the water before continuing diving with tables or another computer. Many authorities recommend that a 24-hour surface interval be observed.

Decompression Software

Several types of decompression software are available. Current systems mainly use a Buhlmann model, modified with gradient factors and micro bubble stops, RGBM, VPM, and AB models. These systems will generally work with any PC (some work on MAC as well).

Various methods are associated with the software. It is recommended that at least one such system be reviewed. For in-depth understanding of decompression models, software programs and dive computers you should complete the IANTD Decompression Software Specialist course. This program is an excellent companion to the one you are currently in.

Gas Management

Gas management is certainly one of the most important factors in diving, especially technical diving. You must have sufficient gas supply to complete the dive as well as provide gas for another diver in an emergency. Consequently, a gas management rule is applied to all technical dives.

Successful gas management requires consistency

Gas Management Rules

Dive Parameters	Rule	Example
• Non-Overhead Environment • No-Stop Dive • <130 fsw/40 msw	**1/2 + 200 Rule**	• Start with 3500 psig • 3500 psig ÷ 2 = 1750 psig • 1750 psig + 200 psig = 1950 psig • Round to nearest 100 psig = 2000 psig • Dive begins return to anchor line or shore at 2000 psig
• Overhead Environment • Decompression Stops Required • > 130 fsw/40 msw • Greater Margin of Safety Required	**Rule of Thirds**	• Start with 3600 psig • 3600 psig ÷ 3 = 1200 psig • 3600 - 1200 = 2400 psig • Diver begins return to anchor line, cave entrance, or shore at 2400 psig

in performance. All divers must maintain a normal respiration rate and swim pace. Keep in mind that gas consumption varies with the individual diver, exertion, thermal and emotional stress. Also, environmental conditions, such as a current, may increase gas consumption. Divers must be prepared to modify the gas management plan accordingly.

When planning decompression gas you must have the amount needed times 1.2 to compensate for anything that may increase your respiration, and also have a reserve gas if you accidentally fall into the next greater schedule. Once the diver's decompression is complete, a buddy or other diver who may have depleted their decompression gas supply can use this additional gas.

Determining Personal Gas Consumption Rates

All divers must know their Respiratory Minute Volume (RMV) in cubic feet per minute (cfm). To find RMV, you must first find your Surface Air Consumption Rate (SAC) as follows:

1. Descend to a depth of 33 fsw (10 msw) and record your cylinder pressure on a slate.
2. Swim at a comfortable pace with a relaxed breathing rate for exactly ten minutes.
3. Document your cylinder pressure at the end of this 10-minute swim and subtract this value from the initial reading.
4. Divide this figure by the depth in atmospheres absolute (in this case, 2).
5. Divide this figure by the swim time (in this case, 10 minutes).

This procedure is expressed in the following formula:

Assume that you consumed 400 psig (25.6 bar)

$$SAC = \frac{\text{Total Gas Consumed (psig / bar)}}{\text{Depth (ata)} \times \text{Time (minutes)}}$$

of air during your 10-minute swim at 33 fsw (10 msw).

Substitute these values:

$$SAC = \frac{400 \text{ psig}}{2 \text{ ata} \times 10 \text{ min}} \qquad SAC = \frac{27.6 \text{ bar}}{2 \text{ ata} \times 10 \text{ min}}$$

SAC = 20 psig/min.   or   SAC = 1.38 bar/min.

Your SAC will vary with cylinder size and working pressure. Consequently, you should convert this value to RMV in order to plan dives using different cylinders. To find your RMV:

1. Divide the rated cylinder working pressure by the rated volume.
2. Divide your SAC by this value (from step 1) to find your RMV.

This procedure may be expressed as follows:

$$RMV = \frac{SAC}{\left(\frac{\text{Rated Cylinder Working Prerssure}}{\text{Rated Cylinder Volume}} \right)}$$

For example, if your SAC was 20 psig and you were using aluminum 80 cf (2266 L) cylinder with a working pressure of 3000 psig, the calculation would be:

$$SAC = \frac{20 \text{ psig / min}}{\left(\frac{3000 \text{ psig}}{80 \text{ cf}} \right)} \qquad SAC = \frac{1.38 \text{ bar / min}}{\left(\frac{209 \text{ bar}}{2266 \text{ liters}} \right)}$$

SAC = 0.53 cfm   or   SAC = 15 liters.

Your SAC value can also be found by consulting the "PSIG/Minute to CF/Minute" table in Appendices B. Keep in mind that the dive may be "controlled" by the team member with the highest RMV and/or the lowest gas volume. You will learn to work with SAC Ratio Factors and Turn Pressure tables in Advanced Deep Air and Technical Nitrox Diver training.

For metric users there is a simpler means of computing cylinder duration. All cylinders are stamped with their volume or water capacity, and all the diver needs to know is their surface liter per minute rate and convert it to depth.

Example: SAC 1.38 x 12L cylinder = 16.56 L/min at the surface x 4 ATA (30 m depth) = 66.24L/min. Thus a 12 L cylinder will last the diver: 12 x 207(rated pressure of cylinder)/ 66.24 = 37.5 minutes

"Successful gas management requires consistency in performance."

Now, let's develop a gas management plan for a dive. The following chart (next page) will take you through the steps for determining gas supply requirements for a team of three divers. Keep in mind the factors that control gas availability and consumption - depth, dive time, RMV, cylinder size, and cylinder pressure.

Factors in Gas Management Planning for No Stop EANx Dives (An Example)

Dive Depth: 100 fsw/30.5 msw		Planned Bottom Time: 30 min		Gas Management: 1/2 + 200	
Item #	Description	Diver 1	Diver 2	Diver 3	
1	Cylinder size in cubic feet (liters)	80 (2266)	100 (2832)	95 (2690)	
2	Cylinder working pressure in psig (bar)	3000 (207)	3500 (241)	2640 (182)	
3	Cylinder fill pressure in psig (bar)	3000 (207)	3000 (207)	2500 (172)	
4	Gas available in cubic feet (liters)(a)	80 (2266)	**85.7 (2427)**	**90 (2549)**	
5	RMV in cubic feet/min (liters/min)	0.50 (14.2)	0.65 (18.4)	0.70 (19.8)	
6	Dive depth in fsw (msw)	100 (30.5)	100 (30.5)	100 (30.5)	
7	Consumed at depth in cfm (lpm)(b)	2.0 (56.8)	2.6 (73.6)	2.8 (79.2)	
8	Bottom time in minutes	30	30	30	
9	Total gas consumption at depth in cubic feet (liters)	60 (1704)	78 (2208)	84 (2376)	
10	Reserve required in cubic feet (liters) using 500 psig(34.5 bar) rule	13.3 (377)	14.3 (405)	18 (510)	
11	Total gas required for Dive in cubic feet (liters)	73.3 (2081)	**92.3 (2613)**	**102 (2886)**	
12	Sufficient gas available	Yes	*No*	*No*	
13	Adjusted Dive Time in Minutes	**25**	**25**	**25**	
14	New total gas consumption at depth in cubic feet (liters)	50 (1470)	65 (1840)	70 (1980)	
15	New total gas required (10+14) in cubic feet (liters)	63.3 (1847)	79.3 (2245)	88 (2490)	
16	Turn pressure in psig (bar)	1700 (117)	1700 (117)	1450 (100)	

(a) Use "Gas Volume vs. Cylinder Pressure Table"

(b) Use "Estimated Gas Consumption Based on Depth & Respiratory Minute Volume Table"

In the example we learned the following:

1. Dives are not always "controlled" by the individual with the smallest cylinder.

2. Cylinders filled to less than rated pressure may compromise the dive plan.

3. If the 500 psig reserve rule commonly used in recreational is applied, the actual reserve air volume will vary with cylinder size. Would there be sufficient gas to assist a fellow diver in an emergency near the end of the dive? Since this is a no-stop, open water dive the supply would be adequate. This might not be the case for a dive requiring decompression or a penetration dive.

Never hesitate to adjust the dive plan to a more conservative level.

5. Turn pressure varies with cylinder pressure. In IANTD's Technical Diving programs, you will learn how to adjust your turn pressure in accord with varying cylinder size and RMV of your dive buddies.

The importance of proper gas management cannot be over-emphasized. As a diver exploring deeper depths or doing longer dives you are developing the knowledge and skills to provide the foundation of a technical diver.

Equipment Management

Each diver is responsible for selecting and assembling *appropriate* personal equipment. The following must be considered for an ocean or open water dive:

- Each diver must have a sufficient volume of

gas to complete the planned dive and meet the reserve requirements as specified above. Keep in mind that you must maintain a sufficient volume of reserve gas to provide another diver with gas during ascent and decompression. This reserve volume must be based on the dive team member with the highest Surface Air Consumption (SAC). Divers may use either a single cylinder or dual cylinder unit as long as it is of sufficient volume to meet these requirements.

- Although teamwork is fundamental to safe diving, Advanced EANx Divers must also develop self-sufficiency. They must be capable independently dealing with equipment failures. For example, the common recreational scuba diving practice of connecting two, second stages to a single first stage regulator is considered inappropriate. Whether diving with single or dual cylinders, the valve or manifold system must accommodate two separate regulators that may be independently controlled. In the event one regulator begins to free-flow, the diver can now isolate it without affecting the gas supply to the remaining regulator.

- Each diver must be equipped with complete instrumentation. A diver must not rely on a buddy's computer or timer to provide critical information. For example, a diver that becomes separated from the rest of the team in limited visibility or is carried away by current must be equipped to independently complete a proper ascent.

- Each diver must have appropriate dive information (i.e., decompression) recorded on a slate. Do not rely on another diver to supply such information underwater.

- Each diver must be capable of independently controlling ascent and maintaining decompression depth in open water. This means that each diver must have a lift bag and line reel.

Summary

Methodical dive planning is essential in advanced EANx and technical diving. In addition to the basic dive planning, a complete advanced EANx or technical dive plan must include oxygen management, inert and overall gas management, and equipment planning.

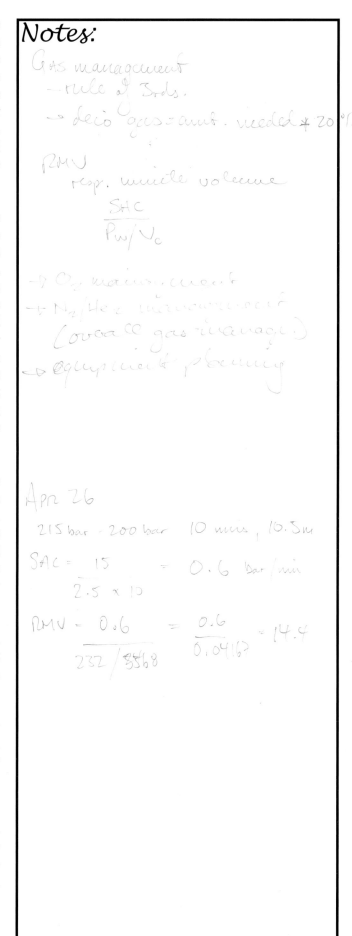

When selecting diving equipment, one must consider both present and future needs. Advanced EANx or Advanced Recreational Trimix Diver training are prerequisites to technical diving. Equipment to be used at this level of training will be more strigent than for normal sport diving applications. In the Advanced Nitrox and Advanced Recreational Trimix Diver courses there is more emphasis on safety, self-sufficiency, and utility, due to the introduction of decompression and gas switching combined with greater flexibility in dive gas. The primary scuba for today may be the "stage" scuba for tomorrow. Keep in mind that future diving may include shipwreck and cave penetrations. Through careful planning and selection, the diver can assemble a state-of-the-art diving configuration that provided the flexibility to grow as the diving interest changes. During this course you will be discussing personal equipment requirements in more detail with your instructor. Furthermore, you are encouraged to consult with an equipment specialist at a dive shop that caters to technical divers.

Primary Equipment

Proper equipment selection and configuration are among the most important aspects of scuba diving. For diving to depths between 140 fsw and 150 fsw (42 msw and 45 msw) must include:

- Scuba cylinder(s) equipped with a dual outlet valve or manifold with gas capacity sufficient to conduct dives applying the appropriate gas management rules; this may be in the form of large capacity single cylinders or double cylinders.

- Two regulators, one with a standard hose and one with a retainer to attach around the divers neck or to the BCD. A second regulator with a second stage on a minimum five foot long hose. One of

An example of a CCR Tek Lite gear configuration. Photo by Jeffrey Bozanic.

An example of a Open Circuit Tek Lite gear configuration. Photo by Jeffrey Bozanic.

these must include a submersible pressure gauge (SPG).

- For open circuit, a regulator with SPG and auxiliary gas source (stage cylinder).

- For rebreathers, a regulator with a SPG and auxiliary gas source (bailout cylinder).

- The diver may opt to use a rebreather in this course in leu of OC SCUBA, in which case it must be an approved system. Talk to your instructor about the options.

- Buoyancy control device (BCD).

- Harness assembly (may be integrated with BCD).

- Dive timer and depth gauge or computer; ideally a multi-gas switch dive computer, or one for closed circuit rebreather (CCR) that uses a constant PO_2 function.

- Dive tables featuring a gas switch to EAN 50 as

A submersible pressure gauge with depth indicator.

the primary decompression reference or as a back up to a dive computer, or for CCR constant PO$_2$ Dive Tables.

- Cutting device.

- Environmental protection appropriate for dive site conditions.

- Slate and pencil.

- Other equipment appropriate to the diving environment as designated by your instructor.

Mask and Fins

Mask and fins selection is a matter of personal preference and comfort. Emphasis is placed on high-quality equipment that fits. A compact and lightweight

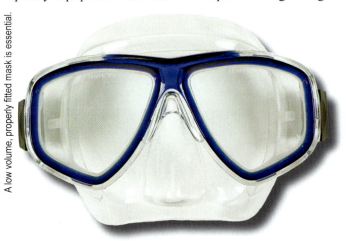

A low volume, properly fitted mask is essential.

mask with a low profile is advantageous, especially when diving in a current. As a diver evolves toward tech diving, there is an ever increasing need for reading gauges, timers, and dive information printed on slates. Some divers requiring vision correction may consider special lenses to facilitate reading small number displays underwater. Various magnifiers and bifocal adaptations are available.

Select fins that combine comfort and performance.

Fins should provide maximum forward thrust with the least amount of energy expended by the diver. Blade size and stiffness must complement diver strength and stature. Either excessively stiff or flexible fins can lead to leg cramps and/or fatigue under demanding diving conditions. Special attention is given to strap attachment mechanisms; a lost fin can severely compromise a diver's safety.

Buoyancy Control Device

Buoyancy control devices (BCD) have undergone considerable evolution over the past decades. The jacket-style BCD has dominated conventional recreational diving, and the back-mount has proven to be most compatible for the challenges of Advanced and technical diving.

Divers aspiring to advance to technical diving are well advised to consider the advantages of back-mounted BCD's. A properly designed back-mounted BCD keeps the lift (i.e. buoyancy) in line with the scuba cylinder(s) to provide stability and maintain the body in a proper swimming position. Initially, a diver

using a single cylinder may select a compact, low profile BCD of relatively low volume (i.e., 20 to 40 pounds/9 to 18 kilograms of lift). As the diver advances to more demanding advanced diving, the compact BCD may be delegated to backup status and replaced by a higher capacity primary unit. Keep in mind that many of the arguments against back-mounted BCD's of decades past have been invalidated by modern trends in BCD design.

In selecting a BCD, a diver must consider both present and future scuba configurations. For example, a 71.2 cf (2,016 l) cylinder that is neutrally buoyant when empty will be about 5.25 pounds (2.38 kg) negative when filled. The diver will have to compensate for the slightly heavier cylinder weight at the beginning of the dive plus any additional buoyancy loss associated with suit compression.

Harness and Back-plates

Some companies produce modular BCD systems that may be custom designed to the diver's stature and needs. In addition, quick-release weight systems may now be integrated into the BCD system. Several systems may be customized and updated as the diver advances to more demanding diving pursuits. A diver may elect to acquire a back plate, harness, weight system, single cylinder mounting plate, utility pocket, and a compact BCD. Later, the diver could add double cylinder bands and a larger capacity primary BCD.

The harness and back plate must hold the cylinder(s) secure, stable, and even on the divers back. The harness must be designed for easy donning, doffing, and adjustment as well as attachment of various accessories. Technical diving harnesses are usually designed to hold the scuba tank more securely to the diver. Velcro waist bands are replaced and/or complemented with straps and buckles for greater security. Weight pockets or pouches are designed for quick-release of block or shot pouch weights. Weight pockets may be loaded differentially to balance the diver's weight needs.

Ballast Systems

Divers often require ballast or weights to overcome natural and equipment-related buoyancy. The most common source of buoyancy is the environmental protection garment. Selecting an appropriate ballast system is much a manner of personal preference. Traditionally, divers have used a web belt fitted with lead weights and a quick-release buckle. Today, increasing numbers of divers integrate ballast into BCD and harness units, as discussed previously. Many divers select scuba cylinders with specific buoyancy and weight characteristics that eliminate the need for supplemental ballast. In this case, the weight is distributed more comfortably and evenly on the diver.

In traditional scuba diving, the ability to drop a separate weight belt is considered as a diver rescue option. Keep in mind that "dropping the weight belt and ascending to the surface" in an emergency *is not* generally a viable option for the technical diver.

Scuba Cylinder

Cylinders for scuba diving are available in volumes ranging from approximately 45 to 125 cubic feet (cf) (7 to 19 liters). Small, auxiliary or "pony" cylinders range from 13 to 45 cf (2 to 7 liters). In selecting a scuba cylinder a diver must consider the following:

Tank bands come in a variety of size ranges.

- What is the maximum intended diving depth and duration (gas volume required)?

- What is the environmental protection garments (buoyancy characteristics)?

- What are the ballast requirements?

- What is the diver's stature? (Long cylinders on short divers are awkward.)

- What is the maximum weight of cylinder or cylinder assembly that the diver can handle?

- Will the cylinder be prepared for high oxygen service? (Steel cylinders with lower pressure ratings are preferable.)

A diver intending to presently dive in the range of 60 to 150 feet (18 to 45 m) and later advance to technical Diver, or Normoxic Trimix, or Trimix diving would be better served by a single 95 to 125 cf (15 to 19 liters) cylinder. The Advanced EANx or Advanced Recreational Trimix Diver will be well served by a single large capacity scuba cylinder. However, a prudent diver will select the cylinder to satisfy both present and future diving needs.

Cylinder Valves & Manifolds

Modular valve systems enable the diver to change valve configurations when advancing to more serious technical diving. A modular valve system may be expanded as follows:

- *Basic "K" valve* is for single cylinder use in less than 60 fsw (18 msw).

- *Basic "K" valve with "H" valve adapter* converts the single "K" valve to a dual outlet [for primary and backup regulators] valve for a single cylinder to be used in overhead environments such as wreck and cave and for greater depths. The advantage of this valve configuration is either regulator may be independently isolated if there is a malfunction.

- *Two basic "K" valves with crossbar* - expands two single cylinders to a dual scuba cylinder with two regulator outlets [primary and backup] for advanced technical diving.

- *Two basic "K" valves with an isolation crossbar* - expand two single cylinders to a dual scuba cylinder with the ability to isolate either cylinder for advanced technical diving.

In addition to providing considerable versatility, the diver will recognize substantial monetary savings by not having to buy a new valve unit as equipment needs change. It should also be noted that several manufacturers supply a "Y" valve to facilitate the use of dual regulators on a single cylinder. Either regulator may be independently isolated in the event of a malfunction. However, the "Y" valve cannot be expanded to a dual cylinder configuration.

Traditionally, the American Scuba Industry has used a standard scuba yoke connector [CGA850 or CGA855 connection]. The yoke system is, however, technically

Valves and manifolds come in yoke and DIN versions.

limited to 3,000 psig under Compressed Gas Association guidelines. For higher pressures, the DIN447 300 bar connector has become the standard fitting. The DIN connector features a "trapped" O-ring configuration that virtually eliminates the potential problem of blown O-rings that occasionally occurs with yoke fittings.

Today, many advanced divers use the more dependable DIN valve for both high and low pressure cylinders. Most regulators are now available with either yoke or DIN connectors. Several manufacturers have DIN cylinder valves with adapters for use with conventional yoke regulators. Advanced EANx and Advanced Recreational Trimix Divers are encouraged to consider the DIN system when selecting cylinder valves.

Regulator

Most regulator manufacturers now supply nitrox compatible regulators and /or special conversion kits that include oxygen compatible o-rings and lubricant. As previously stated, consider both present and future needs when selecting diving equipment.

Your first concern is *performance*. Will the regulator deliver a sufficient volume of gas with minimal breathing effort under high work loads at the anticipated maximum dive depth? Keep in mind that your gas flow requirements can more than quadruple in a high stress situation. If applicable, will the regulator perform adequately in cold water or will it ice [resulting in free-flow] under high demand conditions?

Next, consider *reliability*. Does the regulator have a proven record of reliable performance within your intended application parameters? A reliable equipment dealer and your instructor should be able to assist you in identifying both desirable and undesirable regulators. Regulator *maintainability* is another important consideration. Some regulators require complex and expensive maintenance procedures. Others are very simple to maintain. Since regulators used for deeper or more strenuous diving must always operate at the highest level of performance, maintainability is an important consideration.

Some dives require several hours breathing from regulators. Consequently, a regulator must be *physically comfortable*. Weight and design characteristics become very important in reducing jaw fatigue. Finally, a regulator must be *compatible* with your scuba system. Obvious compatibility requirements include DIN connectors. Less obvious considerations include the physical size of the first stage relative to present and future valve and manifold configurations.

Divers using rebreathers must be even more aware of mouthpiece comfort due to the probability of doing longer dive times as well as the weight of the hoses and mouthpiece itself.

Dive Instruments

A scuba diver must monitor specific information in order to properly execute a safe underwater excursion. First, the diver must be continuously aware of the amount of breathing gas remaining in the scuba cylinder(s). Secondly, the diver must be able to compute that amount of nitrogen that has been absorbed. This can be accomplished by accurately determining maximum depth and exposure time and consulting dive tables or by a diver-carried computer which automatically reads depth (pressure) and time and, using a mathematical model of the human body, determines gas absorption status. In both cases the diver is informed of no-decompression time or decompression time requirements. Finally, the diver must be capable of determining direction and navigating an appropriate course underwater using a compass.

Accurate depth measurement is extremely important for nitrox and decompression diving. Inaccurate depth readings could result in selecting the wrong decompression schedule or exceeding oxygen limits. Divers are encouraged to consult information booklets supplied with depth gauges in order to determine the gauge accuracy. The introduction of electronic instrumentation has significantly improved the accuracy of depth measurement. Depth is measured using a temperature compensated pressure transducer. The pressure reading is converted into a voltage reading and this reading is then processed by the analog-to-digital converter which changes it into

> "Most regulators are now available with either yoke or DIN connectors. Several manufacturers have DIN cylinder valves with adapters for use with conventional yoke

a digital signal that can be displayed or "read" by the microprocessor. Accuracy of electronic or digital depth gauges is either expressed in "±" number of feet or percentage of full scale. For example, most of today's dive computers specify a depth measurement accuracy of ± 1 to 2 feet or ± 1%. Analog depth gauges and any depth gauge that has been subjected to abuse or gives a significantly different reading than those of fellow divers must be tested, repaired, and/or replaced. Consult the manufacturer's instruction booklet or a technical diving service center for additional information.

A water-resistant watch or timer is essential to the scuba diver for determining bottom time, controlling rate of ascent, timing decompression stops, and navigation procedures. Digital watches are often selected for technical diving. Digital watches incorporate a number of features such as time, day, and date function, stop watch, count down timer, alarm functions, and face illumination. Various watch and timing functions are initiated by activating a button on the side of the watch. The stop watch function is valuable for timing both bottom time and decompression stop time. Depth rated or water resistant should be at least 200 meters (660 feet). A dive watch (or timer) must be highly water resistant, reliable, accurate, robust, capable of withstanding thermal stress, readable under a variety of conditions, and capable of standing up to normal dive use.

Divers commonly use a liquid-filled *magnetic compass* for underwater direction finding and navigation. Generally, the compass is part of the instrument console that is attached to the scuba regulator. However, some divers will secure the compass to their wrist or to a compass board. A diver's compass should have the following features: (1) correct dampening action, (2) be liquid filled, (3) a compass rose marked in degrees, (4) lubber line showing direction over the face, (5) a course setting line or reference markers, and (6) a movable bezel. A good compass will respond rapidly to even slight course changes and have a high degree of luminescence for use in dark water.

Dive Computers

Modern dive computers are truly marvelous instruments. The computer consists of a power source, a pressure transducer, an analog to digital converter, an internal clock, a microprocessor (with both ROM and

RAM), and a display screen. Depending on the make and model, the computer is activated (or powered up) by a manual switch, scuba cylinder pressure, or contact with water. Once activated it automatically checks all of its computing circuits and sequentially lights all segments of the screen (and warning lights) to verify that they are working. Some models then display battery voltage. The computer reads and displays ambient "surface reference pressure" in feet or meters of sea water. Some computers will automatically adjust for diving at altitude.

Computers specifically programmed for use with nitrox and trimix as well as constant PO_2 for CCR are currently available. Both independent and gas supply integrated models are available. In addition, some models enable the diver to select a percentage of conservatism ranging from 0 to 50%.

There are several options for mixed gas and multi-gas switch computers.

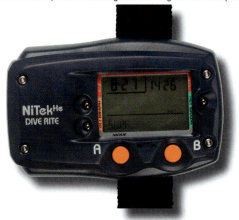

Most computers will now display a *scrolling dive table* which gives the no-decompression dive time at 10 foot (3 meter) depth intervals over a range of depths. When you submerge, the computer's internal timer automatically activates in the dive timing mode and changes in pressure are measured by the pressure transducer. *Dive time and depth* are shown on the display. This information is entered into the microprocessor where it is integrated with stored information (for repetitive dives) and a mathematical model that simulates nitrogen absorption and elimination rates in various theoretical tissue compartments. Using this information the computer displays *remaining no-decompression time*. The computer updates diver status approximately every three seconds taking into account depth changes and diver on-gassing and off-gassing. Air-integrated dive computers that connect to your regulator and read gas supply pressure also estimate and display the remaining amount of dive time available based on present gas consumption.

Most computers will also warn the diver if the programmed ascent rate is exceeded. In the event that the diver remains at depth for a sufficient enough time to exceed the no-decompression limit of the model, a *ceiling depth* is displayed. This is the shallowest depth to which the diver can safely ascend. The diver must stop at or below this depth to allow for nitrogen off-gassing or decompression.

When you reach the surface your computer switches to a surface mode to provide you with the maximum depth and duration of the previous dive (some units scroll the three previous dives), surface interval time, and a scrolling dive table indicating no-decompression time allowance for a repetitive dive. In addition, many computers display a numerical value or a symbol indicating the time that you must wait before flying. Your computer also stores a series of dive profiles. This dive log can be accessed manually or, for some models, downloaded into a desktop computer.

All divers must remember that any mechanical/electronic device is subject to failure or malfunction. Most frequently these failures are a result of human error, carelessness, or physical abuse. A microprocessor will fail if the battery compartment floods because the diver did not clean the o-ring or properly close the compartment. Many divers carry two computers.

Dive computers should never be left in direct sunlight or exposed to potentially high temperature environments. This could result in display fading and damage to electronic components. Following each dive the computer should be rinsed in fresh water. The computer must be protected from excessive shock. Take care in handling computers to avoid dropping or striking against solid objects. Secure the computer so that it does not "drag" across rocks and coral as you swim underwater.

Batteries should be replaced when low power warnings are displayed. Some models are designed for diver battery replacement and others must be returned to an authorized service center. Manufacturer manuals give detailed information on maintenance of specific computers.

Instructions for the use of specific dive computers are beyond the scope of this manual. Divers purchasing computers must read instruction manuals in detail and, ideally, obtain instruction in the use of the computer from a qualified instructor.

Cutting Devices

All divers must be equipped with a knife or suitable cutting device. Entanglements in nylon guidelines, monofilament fish line, or fish nets can be life threatening. A compact, sharp knife with a line cutting

Your equipment configuration must include a cutting tool.

notch is suitable for most diving. The skydiver's hook or z-knife is also popular. Many public safety divers and shipwreck divers carry heavy-duty EMS scissors capable of cutting line and wire. These scissors can also be used for cutting the eye-end from an embedded fishhook to facilitate removal. Cutting devices are carried in suitable scabbards or pouches and may be secured to the scuba harness or strapped to the diver's arm. Many divers carry more than one cutting device variously placed for easy access.

Auxiliary Equipment

In order to deploy and control a line and float for independent decompression in open water, a diver must carry a *small line reel*. Reels are available in a variety of sizes and configurations but all share several key components – a handle, line spool, line guide, winding knob, lock-down nut, and clip. The spool should accommodate a sufficient amount of No. 36 braided nylon line to allow for

deployment of a lift bag from your deepest stop depth. With a sufficient amount of line, this reel may also be used as a wreck penetration reel.

A *scuba diver's liftbag or submersible marker buoy* with a lift capacity to float the diver in even of BC failure is satisfactory for controlling drift decompressions. The bag, constructed of rugged, brightly colored vinyl or nylon, is open at one end and fitted with a bridle and a ring or hook.

One or more small *plastic slates* should be available for recording

An example of a primary reel.

critical dive plan information such as depth, time, decompression schedules, turn pressure and for communicating with fellow divers under water. A standard #2 wood-like pencil may be secured to the slate with rubber tubing. Slates may be clipped to your BCD/ scuba harness or carried in an accessory pocket.

A *jon line* is a 5 foot (1.5 meter) or longer piece of nylon line or webbing fitted with a clip and hand loop. The jon line is secured to an anchor line or hang line to facilitate decompression in ocean currents.

All divers are encouraged to assemble a small, *spare parts/tool kit* with an assortment of straps, clips, rubber tubing, o-rings, screw drivers, wrenches, etc. that might be needed to make minor equipment repairs in the field.

Equipment Configuration

Once you have selected the appropriate equipment, it must be configured for optimal safety and diver performance. First, equipment placement must be *simple* and *clean.* Equipment must be placed on the diver in a *streamlined* fashion to *minimize drag* or resistance to moving through the water. The equipment must be *balanced* to distribute weight and bulk evenly on the diver. Second, the equipment position must be *standardized* and all items must be readily *accessible* and *identifiable* by touch. The diver must be able to reach and operate all valves underwater. Your dive buddy must also be able to access all of your equipment. In other words, the equipment configuration must be *user friendly*. Third, certain items may be *redundant*. Regulator redundancy becomes increasingly important at depths greater than 60 fsw (18 msw). Technical divers also utilize redundant lights [cave and wreck divers], BCD's, cutting devices, and computers. Keep in mind that you are now being trained for self-sufficient diving and *self-rescue*. However, divers are cautioned to avoid excessive redundancy. The following should be considered in configuring your personal diving outfit:

- The diver should breath from the primary regulator and be prepared to hand it off to a out of air diver in an emergency. This second stage should have a five foot hose attached to it.

- The auxiliary regulator must be secured in a visible position on the divers chest. This is usually secured beneath the neck by an elastic cord or strap.

- BCD hoses must be secured to the scuba harness or BCD with an elastic strap or special loop. The BCD valve system must be immediately accessible and cannot be allowed to float above the diver.

- The scuba tank and BCD must be secured comfortably and snugly to the divers body. The scuba tank and BCD should not float off the diver's back when air is placed in the BCD.

- All gauges may be clipped to appropriate rings on the harness or BCD. Gauges must not be allowed to drag beside or below the diver where they can be damaged by impact, catch on obstacles, or damage the environment.

- Cutting devices must be placed where they are readily accessible with either hand and in any position. Favored positions are on the scuba harness and arm; carrying a knife on the lower leg is less desirable. If a knife is carried on the lower leg, it should be on the inside of the leg.

Equipment and Oxygen

All cylinders should be compatible for the gases to be used in them. Any cylinder with EAN 40 or above must be rated for oxygen service. All cylinders must be labeled as to gas content and the MOD of the mix in the cylinders. Nitrox cylinders with up to 40% should be labeled with a normal nitrox label and contents sticker. Cylinders may also be marked with a general trimix label, provided the cylinder also has a contents sticker with the exact mix in the cylinder.

Oxygen Compatibility

There are basically three standards of care that relate to equipment's suitability for use with high-pressure/high-percentage oxygen mixtures. First, the equipment must be free of substances that may fuel a fire or explosion. All equipment components that will be exposed to high-pressure oxygen must be specially cleaned with an appropriate solvent and/or detergent to remove all traces of contamination and then inspected using black-lights and other methods to verify the complete absence of contaminants. Some of the contaminants found in scuba equipment are hydrocarbons and silicon-based lubricants, machining oils, thread lubricants, solvents, metal particles, rust, dust, thread sealant, and lint. Any of these could be significant in the combustion reaction. Once this cleaning process has been completed, the equipment is considered *oxygen clean.* Keep in mind that new scuba equipment is not necessarily oxygen clean. Some manufacturers may ship certain components in an oxygen clean state. These components will be specially labeled and may be sealed in a protective container to prevent contamination during pre-assembly handling.

The next consideration is that non-metallic "soft" components such as o-rings, valve seats and lubricants must be *oxygen compatible.* For example, the buna-N o-rings and silicon lubricants used in most scuba equipment are not oxygen compatible. These components have low auto-ignition temperatures. In order to make a valve or regulator oxygen serviceable, the o-rings must be replaced with ones that are oxygen compatible [i.e., Viton-A o-rings] and the silicon lubricant must be replaced with an oxygen compatible lubricant [i.e., Krytox 240 or Crystolube], as recommended by most manufacturers.

Keep in mind that a component may be oxygen clean but not oxygen compatible and vice versa. For example, a metal cylinder is oxygen compatible, however it may be contaminated. In order to be designated for *oxygen service,* a component must be both oxygen clean and oxygen compatible. This means the component has been properly cleaned, inspected and the components are compatible for use with up to 100% oxygen.

Oxygen and Your Diving Equipment

Can you use ordinary scuba diving equipment with oxygen enriched mixtures? Will oxygen enriched mixtures [up to 40%] lead to accelerated and excessive corrosion or deterioration of equipment? Must equipment

> "Keep in mind... new scuba equipment is not necessarily oxygen clean. Some manufacturers may ship certain components in an oxygen clean state. These components will be specially labeled and may be sealed to prevent contamination during pre-assembly handling."

used with gas mixtures containing oxygen percentages greater than 21% by volume be specially cleaned and modified for oxygen enriched service? Are the lubricants and "soft components" used in the manufacture and maintenance of ordinary scuba diving equipment compatible with oxygen enriched mixtures?

Notes:

With regard to equipment corrosion and deterioration, the following statement is quoted from the SDRG Nitrox Workshop Report: *"Another area about which there has been considerable misunderstanding and misconception is the question of tank corrosion and deterioration of equipment exposed to enriched air mixtures. Experts in the workshop laid this one to rest. There is no noticeable difference in corrosion between a tank containing dry air and one containing dry oxygen enriched air. The same applies to non-metallic components; there is no difference."*

There has been concern regarding handling of oxygen enriched gas mixtures. Some factions of the recreational diving community and the compressed gas industry maintain that any gas mixture containing 23% or greater oxygen by volume (at STP) must be handled as 100% oxygen and that associated equipment must be designed and maintained for oxygen service. On the other hand, organizations such as the National Oceanic and Atmospheric Administration (NOAA) have followed a standard allowing oxygen enriched mixtures up to 40% to be handled essentially the same as air.

The *NOAA Diving Manual*, published in 1991, specifically states: *"High-pressure storage cylinders, scuba tanks, regulators, and all high-pressure gas transfer equipment that is used with pure oxygen or with nitrox mixtures that contain more than 40 percent must be cleaned and maintained for oxygen service."*

The SDRG Nitrox Workshop Report includes the following statement: *"It is well known that mixtures with oxygen in the range of air up to compositions of 40 or 50% are much easier to handle than oxygen, and for the most part can be handled with methods similar to those for air."*

The report states further: *"In fact, several existing standards allow mixtures of up to 40% oxygen to be used with equipment designed for air service, or conversely, mixtures having oxygen percentages above 40% require handling and equipment the same as for oxygen service."*

One of the most significant disclosures in the SDRG Nitrox Workshop Report related to the lubricants used in high pressure gas systems. To quote: *"There is a 'myth' in parts of the recreational diving community that silicone greases are oxygen compatible, whereas in fact they are highly flammable in oxygen, and can initiate fire in an oxygen system of incorrect design and with incorrect handling."*

The report further stated: *"The lubricant in a high pressure gas system containing oxygen is by far the most vulnerable and easily ignited part of the system, but it is also the most easily corrected."*

The Workshop recommended that: "...perfluorinated polyether lubricants [being oxygen compatible lubricants with properties acceptable for diving equipment and conditions] *be used exclusively on diving apparatus. (These lubricants are for the valve, regulator, O-rings, etc., not for the crankcase of a compressor.)*"

This recommendation *implies*, but does not specifically state, that the recommended lubricant be used with all diving apparatus, regardless of breathing mixture.

The Blending Standards of the International Association of Nitrox Divers, Inc./IANTD specifically state: *"Regulators and all equipment exposed to high pressures (pressures in excess of 200 psig) must use oxygen compatible lubricants. If the equipment is used in an environment with greater than 40% oxygen, it must be oxygen service rated."*

Some manufacturers specify that their equipment not be used with enriched air nitrox. Users of oxygen enriched mixtures are encouraged to respect the recommendations of individual manufacturers. In fact, the *Blending Standards of the International Association of Nitrox Divers, Inc./IANTD* specifically state: *"SCUBA equipment used with mixed gases should be done so in accordance with the recommendations of individual manufacturers. If a manufacturer states that their equipment is not compatible with breathing gases other than air, then that brand of equipment should not be used. All modifications of equipment required by a manufacturer for use of their equipment with breathing gases other than air must be performed prior to using that brand of equipment."*

Training for Gas Blenders

Training for gas blenders is a more complex process than can be comprehensively covered in this guide. It forms part of a more extensive IANTD course on gas management and oxygen use. Mixing of oxygen-enriched air should be limited to personnel who have been properly trained in this procedure by a designated organization.

Analyzing Nitrox

Most nitrox vendors require customers to analyze the oxygen percentage of the mixture in the cylinder after filling (or before rental) and document the analysis in a Fill Station Log Book with date and signature. Consequently, every nitrox diver must be capable of analyzing a gas mixture for percent oxygen. This is a very simple

procedure and an excellent safeguard to reduce the risk of using an improperly mixed cylinder of gas. Keep in mind that the analysis must be within ±1% for the use of nitrox tables. For example, the EAN 32 Table can be used only with a mixture where the oxygen level is in the range of 31-33%. If the oxygen level is higher, the diver must make adjustments to minimize the risk of oxygen toxicity. On the other hand, if the oxygen level is lower, the diver will have to make adjustments to minimize the risk of decompression sickness.

Each time the analyzer is used it must be *calibrated*. To calibrate the analyzer, turn on the unit while it is exposed to *a flow* of atmospheric air and wait at least one minute or until the digital reading has stabilized. If the display reading is other than 20.8 to 21%, adjust the reading using the calibration dial. If the reading cannot be adjusted to this level, the instrument is malfunctioning and must be serviced. The sensor consists of two electrodes - a cathode and an anode. The gold cathode is exposed to the atmosphere through a fluoropolymer membrane. The lead anode is submerged in potassium hydroxide solution. When oxygen diffuses through the membrane, the electrochemical reduction of oxygen on the cathode and the corresponding oxidation of the anode

> ## "Each time the analyzer is used it must be calibrated. If the display reading is other than 20.8% to 21%, adjust the reading using the calibration dial. If the reading cannot be adjusted to this level, the instrument is malfunctioning and

Always keep a variety of replacement components in your dive bag.

generates an electrical current proportional to the partial pressure of oxygen in the sample gas. The resulting current is monitored, temperature compensated, and amplified to drive the display.

In more sophisticated systems a pressure regulator fitted with a flow meter is used to regulate the flow of nitrox past a galvanic oxygen sensor. The regulator is attached to your scuba cylinder valve the same as attaching a scuba regulator. The sensor is fitted into an accumulator tube that is attached to the flow meter. The flow rate is adjusted to approximately 2 liters per minute. The digital display will steadily increase and within 10 to 30 seconds stabilize at a specific reading. This reading is the percentage of oxygen in your breathing mixture.

Portable oxygen analyzers used by technical divers generally have an accuracy of ±1% of full scale and the sensor element has an operational life of approximately 3 years in air. Sensors retained in a sealed container, as shipped, will generally have a minimum shelf life of 3 months without degradation of life. Each oxygen analyzer is shipped with an operating and maintenance manual. *Users must read this manual completely prior to using the analyzer.* Initial setup involves inserting a 9-volt alkaline battery, attaching a cable, and attaching the oxygen sensor to the cable.

The oxygen analyzer and sensor must be handled with care. The unit can be damaged by physical abuse. Furthermore, care must be taken to prevent exposure to moisture. If moisture condenses on the diffusion membrane of the sensor face, the oxygen path is physically blocked and a lower oxygen concentration is indicated. Occasionally, water may be present in the outer portion of the scuba valve orifice [moisture accumulation resulting by exposing a non-protected orifice to atmospheric precipitation or careless introduction after filling the cylinder in a water bath]. This moisture may be unexpectedly blown on to the sensor.

The oxygen sensor is desensitized to temperature changes by the use of a thermistor located within the sensor. Although some variation in sensor readings may occur with changes in temperature, using the instrument at or close to the same temperature at which it was calibrated minimizes this variation. Users are cautioned to limit handling of the sensor during calibration and use, since body heat can cause the sensor's thermistor to change disproportionate to the change in gas sample temperature at the sensing electrode.

What if you analyze a cylinder of nitrox using two different analyzers and get two significantly different readings (greater than 1% variation)? Since either of the analyzers could be in error, ideally you should analyze the gas with a third analyzer. It is probably safe to assume that the two analyzers that most closely agree are correct. However, what if you do not have a third analyzer available? Could you still use the cylinder of nitrox for the dive? Let's assume that the readings varied by 3 or 4 percent. For example, you purchased a cylinder of 32% nitrox and at the time of purchase you analyzed it at 32.1% oxygen. Using a second analyzer at the dive site, the oxygen read as 35.6%. The following procedure could be used:

1. Assume that either analyzer could be *either* correct *or* faulty.

2. Use the *highest* oxygen reading to determine the maximum dive depth and reduce the risk of oxygen toxicity.

3. Use the highest nitrogen level to determine the maximum no-stop dive time.

4. Dive conservatively!

In the above situation your dive depth would be limited to less than 110 fsw (33 msw) and you would use the EAN 32 dive table to determine maximum no-stop dive time. However, you would dive conservatively without

approaching either limit.

Keeping Records

It is the responsibility of the IANTD fill station to keep a log of any Nitrox they produce. It is your responsibility to ensure that you verify the analysis prior to signing the station logbook and then diving.

Notes:

Chapter 3 - Oxygen
by David Sawatzky, M.D.

Oxygen (O_2) is vital to support human life, but too much or too little oxygen can cause permanent damage and death. Air is 21% oxygen and is toxic at any partial pressure. However, the body has developed very effective mechanisms to handle oxygen toxicity in the gas breathed by the partial pressure of oxygen (PO_2). Toxic effects are only seen when the PO_2 rises above normal. The recent resurgence of hyperbaric oxygen therapy, increased use of oxygen during decompression, rising use of Nitrox in diving, and aggressive use of oxygen in intensive care units has resulted in many people being exposed to increased PO_2. Therefore, practical experience with increased PO_2 is accumulating rapidly. Scientists have recently learned that oxygen toxicity is a major component of the damage mechanism in a number of non-diving diseases (reperfusion injury), and there has been a dramatic expansion of research into oxygen toxicity.

Because of the unique way in which oxygen binds to hemoglobin, there is very little reduction in the amount of oxygen delivered to the tissues until the inspired PO_2 falls below 0.16 ATA. This is fortunate because as we ascend to altitude, the atmospheric pressure and PO_2 fall. At a PO_2 of 0.15 ATA, most individuals will become dizzy with heavy work and at a PO_2 of 0.10 ATA; most individuals will have problems even at rest. At PO_{2s} of less than 0.10 ATA almost everyone will be unconscious and at lower levels will die. For individuals with significant lung damage (e.g., people who smoked more than 1+ pack of cigarettes daily for 10 years, or equivalent), the effects of not enough oxygen (hypoxia) will become noticeable sooner and at higher partial pressures.

The bow of the Saganaga. Photo by Greg Lawlor.

Oxidation

The only common situation where recreational divers must worry about hypoxia is when they have left a tank of air sit for a long time and there is water in the tank. The water causes oxidation. *Oxidation* is the process where the oxygen in the air combines with the metal in the tank, resulting in tank damage and less oxygen in the air. Both aluminum and steel tanks oxidize. In aluminum tanks, the oxidized layer coats the inside of the tank and prevents the underlying aluminum from coming into contact with the air. In steel tanks, the oxidized steel (rust) tends to flake off and continues to expose the underlying steel to air so the process continues. If a steel tank has been left over the winter, there may be no oxygen left in the air. Divers have died using a tank on the first dive in the spring that was filled the previous fall. They almost immediately loose consciousness, usually on the way down when they are negatively buoyant, and drown. I strongly recommend that all divers have VIPs done on their tanks in the winter. The dive stores are less busy and you guarantee that you have clean, dry, good air for the beginning of the spring. Breathing off the tank for a minute beforehand, away from the water, will also tell you if the gas contains sufficient oxygen. Be sure that someone is around to revive you!

Oxygen Toxicity

The human body is able to tolerate increased levels of oxygen, up to about 0.45 ATA, without problem. When the PO_2 rises above that level, toxic effects will eventually appear. At PO_2s of between 0.45 ATA and 1.6 ATA, the toxic effects are mainly on the lungs and take hours or days to develop. At pressure over 1.6 ATA, the toxic effects are mainly on the brain (CNS) and may develop in minutes.

The majority of recreational divers will not have to worry about oxygen toxicity because the PO_2 will never be high enough and long enough to cause problems. The narcotic effect of nitrogen causes divers to limit their depth to a maximum of 130 fsw (40 msw) under ideal conditions at that pressure the PO_2 is just over 1.0 ATA, too low to worry about CNS toxicity. Limited gas supplies keep bottom times short enough that we do not have to worry about lung toxicity. However, the increasing use of oxygen and Nitrox are resulting in some recreational divers being exposed to toxic levels of oxygen. All divers should have a thorough understanding of oxygen toxicity.

Oxygen is a colorless, odorless, tasteless gas and makes up 20.98% of air by volume. The toxicity of oxygen is a function of the PO_2, the time of exposure and individual variation. There is a marked difference in the susceptibility of individuals to oxygen toxicity and a change in the same individual from day to day. The toxicity of oxygen is really a function of the PO_2 in the cells. All cells eventually die if they are exposed to a high enough PO_2 for a long enough time. We only need to be concerned about two tissues, the lungs and brain. The toxic effects of oxygen here will incapacitate us before the other tissues have a problem.

In general, a cell's susceptibility to oxygen toxicity relates to its metabolism rate. A resting cell is relatively resistant. The toxicity of oxygen is not actually due to the oxygen, but oxygen radicals. Oxygen radicals are highly reactive molecules, formed from oxygen, which contain at least one extra electron. Examples include super oxide anions, hydrogen peroxide, hydroperoxy and hydroxyl radicals, and single oxygen. These molecules are formed from collisions between oxygen molecules and as a result of metabolic processes in the cells. They are always forming and cells have processes to deal with them. When the PO_2 is too high however, the number of oxygen radicals being formed is too great, and the cells defenses are overwhelmed, allowing damage.

There are hundreds of specific chemical reactions that oxygen radicals can be involved, which cause cell damage. In general terms there are three ways. First, is through inactivation of enzymes. Enzymes are proteins that work as catalysts, causing reactions to occur that would not normally occur at body temperature. They do this by holding the molecule to react in exactly the right orientation to each other. If the shape of the enzymes is changed, the molecules will not be oriented and the reaction will not occur. Oxygen radicals cause cross-linking of sulphydryl groups, thereby changing the shape of the enzyme and inactivating it. They also cause changes in the shape of the proteins responsible for the transport of ions in and out of the cells across the cell membrane. Finally, oxygen radicals cause peroxidation of the various lipids in the cells.

OXYGEN POISONING

High Inspired Oxygen Pressure

Pulmonary — Neurological — Cellular

Eye Damage - Blood Cell Damage - Liver Damage - Heart Damage - Endocrine Damage - Kidney Damage

Atelectasis
Anoxemia
Acidosis
DEATH

Chemical Toxicity
Cell Destruction
DEATH

Twitching
Convulsions
Neuron Death
DEATH

Artwork: Glenn Forest

All cells in oxygen breathing animals have ways to inactivate oxygen radicals and to repair some of the damage done by them. The two main defenses are super oxide dysmutase and catalase. Both of these enzymes help maintain a good supply of reduced glutathione. Reduced glutathione has many sulphydryl groups and oxygen radicals will bind to them, and thus be unavailable to cause damage to the cell. Dr. J. Lorrain Smith first described the toxic effect of oxygen on the lungs in 1899. He noted that the severity of the effect increased with increasing PO_2 and that the effects where largely reversible. The toxic effect of oxygen on the lungs is primarily a problem of long exposures to PO_2s of between 0.45 and 1.6 ATA. At PO_2s above 1.6 ATA, the toxic effects of oxygen on the brain occur before the toxic effects on the lungs.

The toxic effects of oxygen at partial pressures between 0.45 ATA and 1.6 ATA are primarily on the lungs while the toxic effect at PO_2s over 1.6 ATA are primarily on the brain. The earliest sign of pulmonary (lung) oxygen toxicity is a mild irritation in the trachea (throat) that is made worse with deep inspiration. A mild cough develops next, followed by more severe irritation and cough until inspiration becomes quite painful and the cough becomes uncontrollable. If exposure to oxygen is continued, the person will notice chest tightness, difficulty breathing, shortness of breath, and if exposure is continued long enough, the person will die, from lack of oxygen! The progressive damage to the lungs eventually makes it impossible for the oxygen to get to the blood as it passes through the lungs.

Tracking Oxygen Exposure

The time to onset of symptoms id highly variable

but most individuals can tolerate 12-16 hours of oxygen at 1.0 ATA, 8-14 hours at 1.5 ATA, and 3-6 hours at 2.0 ATA before developing mild symptoms. There are several ways to track developing pulmonary oxygen toxicity but the most sensitive and accurate is the development of symptoms.

A second technique is to monitor the vital capacity. Vital capacity (the amount of air that can be moved in one large breath) decreases with increasing pulmonary toxicity. A reduction of approximately 2% in vital capacity correlates with mild symptoms that are so severe that most individuals will not voluntarily continue breathing oxygen. These mild effects are completely reversible and no permanent lung damage occurs. However, the more severe damage will take up to 12 days to heal. While the pathology of pulmonary oxygen toxicity is understood, it is beyond the scope of this text.

"There is huge variation in the amount of oxygen individuals can tolerate before they show signs of CNS oxygen toxicity and of even more concern, a huge variation in the same person on different days."

A third way to keep track, in rough terms, of pulmonary oxygen toxicity is to keep track of the oxygen exposure. This technique is called calculating the Oxygen Tolerance Units (OTU) and one OTU is equivalent to breathing 100% oxygen, for one minute, at 1.0 ATA. As a guide, 615 OTUs in one day will cause 2% reduction in vital capacity and 1,425 units will cause a 10% decrease. There are several different ways to calculate the OTU (some try to correct for increasing toxic effects with increasing dose, in addition to the simple PO_2 and there is quite wide variation in individual tolerance so that symptoms are still the best guide. The situation where OTUs are most useful is in planning a large number of dives, in a few days, all involving a large amount of oxygen decompression. Even, then the dive plan may have to be altered if the diver develops symptoms of pulmonary toxicity.

Preventing Oxygen Toxicity

The first and most important method to prevent pulmonary oxygen toxicity is to limit exposure to the lowest possible PO_2 for the shortest period of time. If you dive only air and limit your depth to a maximum of 130 fsw (40 msw), pulmonary oxygen toxicity is unlikely to be a problem. The second method to prevent pulmonary oxygen toxicity is to provide air breaks. The damage to the cells is cumulative and if for every 25 minutes of oxygen exposure you provide the cells with a five-minute period where the diver breathes air, the cells can catch-up with the oxygen damage. In experimental situations, the diver can tolerate twice as much oxygen before toxic symptoms develop when air breaks are given compared to breathing oxygen continuously.

Oxygen toxicity on the brain (CNS) is a problem of higher PO_2s for shorter periods of time. While breathing air, a PO_2 of 1.6 ATA is not reached until a depth of 218 fsw (67msw). Therefore, CNS oxygen toxicity is not a problem for standard recreational diving. However, more and more divers are using Nitrox and if you dive breathing a 40% oxygen mixture, the PO_2 will be 1.6 ATA at a depth of only 99 fsw (30 msw) and if you decompress on 100% oxygen, the PO_2 will be 1.6 ATA at a depth of 20 fsw (6 msw)! Therefore, CNS oxygen toxicity is a serious problem for some recreational divers, and a major problem for technical and commercial divers.

Signs & Symptoms

The first and most serious sign of CNS oxygen toxicity is often a grand-mal type of convulsion (i.e. appears similar to a diabetic or epileptic seizure). There are many other signs and symptoms of oxygen toxicity but there is no consistent warning that a seizure is about

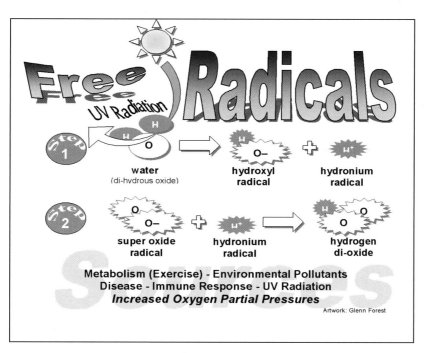

water
(di-hydrous oxide)

hydroxyl radical

hydronium radical

super oxide radical

hydronium radical

hydrogen di-oxide

Metabolism (Exercise) - Environmental Pollutants
Disease - Immune Response - UV Radiation
Increased Oxygen Partial Pressures

Artwork: Glenn Forest

to occur. Even the EEG is completely normal until the convulsion starts. The convulsion due to oxygen toxicity is not believed to cause any permanent problems in and of it self because the body starts to convulsion with a surplus of oxygen on board and thus the hypoxia seen with normal seizures is not a problem. However, the diver who convulses while in the water may drown or, if they ascend while the glottis is closed, may suffer pulmonary barotraumas.

There is huge variation in the amount of oxygen individuals can tolerate before they show signs of CNS oxygen toxicity and of even more concern, a huge variation in the same person on different days. A diver may do many dives in which they are exposed to high PO_2s with no difficulties and falsely conclude that they are resistant to oxygen toxicity. Then, for no apparent reason, they may suffer a CNS hit on a dive where they are exposed to a lower PO_2. In general, people can tolerate more oxygen in a dry chamber than in water.

The acronym for the 7 symptoms of **Oxygen Toxicity** is

CON-VENTID:

- **CON**vulsions
- **V**isual Changes
- **E**uphoria
- **N**ausea
- **T**witching
- **I**rritability
- **D**izziness

In fact, most divers can tolerate two hours of oxygen at 3.0 ATA (66 fsw/20 msw) in a chamber with few difficulties. While exercising in the water however, several divers have convulsed at PO_2s as low as 1.6 ATA. To make matters worse, in the chamber divers often have one of the less serious sign of oxygen toxicity such a tunnel

Diving your Tek Lite gear configuration on recreational dives helps skills stay sharp. Photo by Tom Mount.

vision, ringing in the ears or seizure. The seizure starts with an immediate loss of consciousness and a period of about 30 seconds when the muscles are relaxed. All of the muscles contract violently for about one minute; the diver begins to breath rapidly and is very confused for several minutes afterwards. As you can well imagine, if this happens during a dive, the diver usually dies. The table above gives a short list of the signs and symptoms of CNS oxygen toxicity but almost anything is possible.

Some factors are known to increase the risk of CNS oxygen toxicity. We have already mentioned two, submersion in water and exertion. The risk with working hard is that the PCO_2 in the body increases and this increases the blood flow to the brain. Other causes of increased PCO_2 are skip breathing and increased carbon dioxide in the breathing gas. Added stress on the diver and high levels of adrenaline, atropine, aspirin, amphetamine and other stimulants all seem to increase the risk of CNS oxygen toxicity.

Summary

There are no drugs that can be used to prevent CNS oxygen toxicity. In animal experiments, the seizures could be prevented but CNS cellular damage from prolonged seizures still occurred. The only effective methods to prevent CNS oxygen toxicity are limiting the PO_2, time of exposure, and taking air breaks during oxygen breathing.

As general guidelines, the PO_2 decompression while at rest should never exceed 2.0 ATA and most divers use 100% oxygen at a maximum depth of 20 fsw (6 msw). During the active part of the dive, the PO_2 should never exceed 1.6 ATA and many divers are using 1.5, 1.4, or even 1.3 as the maximum PO_2. NOAA, the US Navy, the Royal Navy, the Canadian Forces, and many other organizations have guidelines for acceptable PO_2s and the maximum time that may be spent at each.

Chapter 4 - Narcosis
by David Doulette, Ph.D.

The narcotic effects of breathing compressed air at depths greater than 100 fsw (30 msw) are probably familiar to most divers. The collection of neurological effects from breathing air at high pressure, including intoxication, slowing of mental processes and reduced manual dexterity are generally referred to as nitrogen narcosis. Such effects occur when breathing many other inert gases in addition to nitrogen, so the condition is more generally known as *inert gas narcosis*. After describing the signs and symptoms of inert gas narcosis, this chapter will show that inert gas narcosis is essentially the effect of anesthesia prior to unconsciousness. Although the underlying mechanisms of narcosis and anesthesia are not completely understood, a number of features of both conditions will be presented, including features other than inert gas partial pressure which modify narcosis.

Historical Descriptions

Intoxication of caisson workers and divers was noted by the middle of the 19th century when engineering advances allowed work at sufficiently elevated pressure. The seminal work describes the narcotic effect of deep air diving dating back to the 1930s. Narcosis was encountered during the first Royal Navy deep air diving trials to 300 fsw (91 msw) and was appropriately described as a "slowing of cerebration" or "as if ... under an anesthetic", but was at that time attributed to "mental instability" in some deep diving candidates (Hill and Phillips, 1932). The role of raised inspired partial pressure of nitrogen in producing narcosis was suspected by 1935, and the use of an alternative breathing gas mixture to eliminate narcosis was proposed (Behnke et al., 1935). Since then, the threshold pressure for air diving that consistently produces a decrement in diver performance has been 4 ATA (100 fsw/30 msw). Confirmation of the role of nitrogen in narcosis came with the report of Max Nohl's 410 ffw (128 mfw) fresh water dive using a Heliox Rebreather of his own design (End, 1938).

Inert Gas Narcosis & Behavioral Modification: Classification of Signs & Symptoms

Inert gas narcosis alters function of the nervous system that produces behavioral modifications, which may impair a diver's ability to work effectively. To recognize all the potential performance impairments resulting from inert gas narcosis and to help understand the causes of narcosis, it is useful to classify the various effects. Behnke originally divided the effects of narcosis into three categories: emotional reactions, impairment of higher mental processes and impairment of neuromuscular control (Behnke et al., 1935). A similar classification is used here: subjective sensations, impaired cognitive function, slowed mental activity and impaired neuromuscular coordination.

Subjective Sensations

Subjective sensations are the sensations that any diver would associate with inert gas narcosis. These include euphoria, intoxication hyper-confidence, recklessness and various altered states of consciousness and attention. Subjective sensations of inert gas narcosis can be assessed using questionnaires asking for a global estimate of the magnitude of narcosis and responses to adjectives, checklists describing work capability (e.g., ability to work, alertness, concentration) and body/mental sensations (e.g., intoxicated, reckless, dreamy, uninhibited). (Hamilton et al., 1992; Hamilton et al., 1995).

Impaired Cognitive Function

Cognitive functions are higher brain processes including perception, thinking, understanding and remembering. The effects of inert gas narcosis on cognitive function includes: difficulty assimilating facts, slowed and inaccurate thought processes, and memory loss. In the laboratory, inert gas narcosis can be measured by tests for impaired cognitive function including: conceptual reasoning, sentence comprehension, mental arithmetic ability, and short-term memory.

The effects of inert gas narcosis on cognitive function includes:
- Difficulty assimilating facts
- Slowed and inaccurate thought processes
- Memory loss

In the laboratory, inert gas narcosis can be measured by tests for impaired cognitive function including:
- Conceptual reasoning
- Sentence comprehension
- Mental arithmetic ability
- Short-term memory

Slowed Mental Activity

In addition to increased errors in cognitive function tests, narcosis significantly reduces the speed at which such problems are solved. Information processing in the central nervous system is slowed and can be

measured in two ways: the rate at which test problems are attempted or reaction time. Reaction time measures the time between receiving a sensory signal and reacting with the appropriate response. It represents the speed of higher mental processes, particularly decision making. Inert gas narcosis slows the reaction time. In a typical laboratory reaction time test one of a series of LEDs is illuminated and the time until it is extinguished by pushing its matched microswitch is measured.

Reduced Neuromuscular Coordination

Neuromuscular coordination (manual dexterity) is impaired by inert gas narcosis but usually only at greater depths than the intellectual impairments described above. Neuromuscular coordination is often assessed by peg board and screw board tests that involve assembly and disassembly of patterns of nuts, bolts and pegs.

Inert Gas Narcosis at Extreme Depth on Air

Air breathing at depths greater than 300 fsw (91 msw) produces altered states of consciousness including manic or depressive states, hallucinations, time disorganization and lapses of consciousness.

Thermoregulation

In addition to the obvious actions of narcosis on brain activity, other body activities are affected as a result of changes in the nervous system. Of particular importance to divers, but less widely known, is the distortion caused by inert gas narcosis of the physiological and behavioral control of body core temperature (i.e. thermoregulation). Narcosis reduces shivering and therefore the production of body heat (i.e. shivering thermogenesis), the main defense against body cooling. As a result, narcosis allows a more rapid drop in body core temperature than expected during cold water. [Mekjavic et al., 1995] Additionally, despite body core cooling, perceived thermal comfort is greater with narcosis than otherwise expected. [Mekjavic et al., 1994] As a result, the diver may neglect to take action to reduce heat loss (i.e. behavioral thermoregulation).

Mechanism of Inert Gas Narcosis Anesthesia

It is apparent that the signs and symptoms of inert gas narcosis result from an alteration of the function of the nervous system. It was noted prior that breathing air at depths greater than 300 fsw (91 msw) produces lapses of consciousness. At much greater depths, air will cause complete unconsciousness (anesthesia). Indeed, many of the inert gases will produce anesthesia, each such gas having a characteristic anesthetic potency. For instance, the approximate inspired partial pressure required to produce anesthesia for nitrogen is 33 ATA, for argon is 15 ATA, for nitrous oxide is 1.5 ATA and for halothane

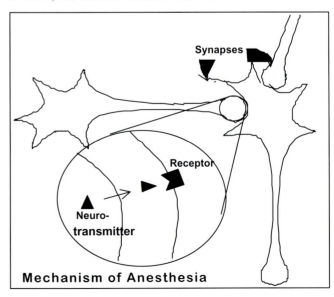

Mechanism of Anesthesia

is 0.008 ATA. [Smith 1986] Some inert gases, notably helium and neon, have no practical anesthetic potency. Owing to its similarity with anesthesia, inert gas narcosis is now generally accepted to be a manifestation of the effects of anesthetic gases at sub-anesthetic doses (i.e. incipient anesthesia). The severity of narcosis increases as the inspired partial pressure of the inert gas approaches the anesthetic level.

Different Inert Gases & Anesthetics Produce Identical Narcosis

The narcotic effects of the inert gases and other anesthetics are identical. In specific test of narcosis in monkeys or humans, argon, nitrogen, nitrous oxide and other general anesthetics have identical effects, although at different partial pressures. Nitrous oxide, which is sufficiently potent to produce narcosis at the surface, has been used extensively in laboratory tests to simulate nitrogen narcosis.

"The severity of narcosis increases as the inspired partial pressure of the inert gas approaches the anesthetic level."

The mechanism by which any anesthetics, including the inert gases, produce anesthesia is not entirely understood. However, it is widely accepted that the site of anesthesia and narcosis are the synapses in the central nervous system. Most drugs, that impact the nervous system, work by modifying the chemical synaptic transmission. Anesthetics enhance the action of a variety of the inhibitory neurotransmitters, particularly GABA, at their specific post-synaptic receptors, resulting in a reduced frequency of action potentials. Such depression of central nervous system activity ultimately produces anesthesia. Synapses carry messages between neurons. Signals in the brain are carried along neurons in the form of an electrical potential called an action potential.

Signals are transmitted across the synapses between neurons by chemicals called neurotransmitters,

Notes:

END

Equivalent Narcotic Depth

$$= (Depth + 10m) \times (1 - PHe) - 10$$

e.g.

$$END_{28/25} = (50 + 10) \times (1 - 0.25) - 10$$
@ 50m
$$= 60 \times 0.75 - 10$$
$$= 35m$$

$$END_{26/25} = 55 \times 0.75 - 10$$
@ 45m
$$= 31.25m$$

$$END = \frac{PN_2 \times depth_{ATA}}{0.79} - 10$$

Notes:

released in response to an action potential. Neurotransmitters combine with specific receptor proteins on the post-synaptic or target neuron. Some neurons release inhibitory neurotransmitters which make the target neuron less likely to fire an action potential while other neurons release excitatory transmitter, which make the target neurons more likely to fire an action potential.

Meyer-Overton Correlation & the Critical Volume Hypothesis

Early hypotheses of anesthetic mechanisms pre-date the discovery of chemical synaptic transmission. The most famous is the Meyer-Overton correlation, which originated at the turn of this century. Meyer [1899] and later Overton [1902] noticed that a remarkably strong correlation exists between an anesthetic's potency and its solubility in olive oil. The Meyer-Overton hypothesis states that anesthesia occurs with certain molar concentration of a compound in the lipid fat of a cell. An elaboration of this hypothesis was proposed by Mullins [1954], and states that narcosis occurs as the volume of some hydrophobic site, probably lipid, expands due to uptake of inert substance [Smith 1986]. It is implied in both these hypotheses that the lipid site is the neuronal cell membrane and that anesthetics work by dissolving in the cell membrane and disrupting the voltage-gated ion channels, which allow the neuron to conduct electrical impulses.

It is no longer widely believed that the membrane voltage-gated ion channels are the sites of anesthesia because evidence has accumulated that any effects of anesthetics on neuronal membranes are physiologically insignificant. Anesthetics may act by occupying hydrophobic pockets inside the neurotransmitter receptor proteins and it is not altogether surprising that a strong correlation exists between anesthetic potency and hydrophobicity. Also, the receptors are embedded in the cell membrane and lipophilic compounds will diffuse rapidly through the membrane and reach high concentration surrounding the receptors. Additionally, lipid soluble compounds readily cross the blood-brain-barrier. So, rather than explaining anesthesia, the Meyer-Overton hypothesis is a useful, incidental relationship. Indeed, it was the low lipid solubility of helium that originally suggested it is tested as a non-narcotic breathing gas diluent. [Behnke, et al., 1935]

Narcosis Slows Mental Processing

Many of the actions of narcosis can be attributed to slow information processing in the central nervous system. The slowed processing model is a useful tool to understand and investigate narcosis [Fowler et al.,

1985]. The slowed processing model suggests that decreased arousal due to the anesthetic properties of inert gases slows the processing of information in the central nervous system and results in the some of the behavioral modifications typical of inert gas narcosis. In order to understand this model one must consider the underlying model of information processing and then how it is affected by narcosis.

decreasing the speed of information handling at any stage impairs performance. Thirdly, the strategy for information handling includes distribution of attention, decision criteria, rehearsal strategies, and speed-accuracy trade-offs.

Functional Component

Slowed processing of information due to inert gas narcosis is evident in laboratory tests of cognitive

Bombs on the USS Saratoga. Photo by Fabio Amaral.

Information Processing Model

Information processing occurs in a series of stages. For instance, a simple information processing task, such as a reaction time, involves a perceptual and evaluation stage, a decision making stage and an effector stage. An example of a reaction time is the delay between seeing a red stop light while driving and applying the brakes. Recognizing a red stop light amongst the thousands of other stimuli occurs in the perceptual and evaluation stage; the decision whether or not to brake, involving calculating speed, distance and chance of a collision, occurs in the decision making stage. Activating the neuromotor programs to operate the leg muscles occurs in the effector stage. There are three aspects of such a system that could be influenced by narcosis. The first one is the structure of the system. Each stage occurs in a different brain area and narcosis could disturb those areas. Secondly, the functional aspect of this model is the overall performance of the system due to the speed of information processing at each stage. Within limits,

function where the number of problems attempted is reduced [Hesser, et al., 1978; Fothergill, et al., 1991] and in increased reaction time [Hamilton, et al., 1995; Fowler, et al., 1986; Fowler et al., 1993]. Considerable experimental data indicates that narcosis produces a general functional deficit rather than distorting the structural components. [Fowler, et al., 1986; Fowler, et al., 1985.] This functional deficit can be explained as slowed processing at any of the stages owing to decreased arousal (i.e. decreased general level of brain activity) or reduced activation (i.e. reduced readiness for activity). It is now thought that narcosis may influence multiple processing stages. Reaction time tests, in combination with recording of brain electrical events indicate that slowed processing by narcosis seems to involve both slowing of the perceptual evaluation stage and also reduction of motor readiness at a later effect or stage. [Fowler, et al., 1993]. The notion of narcosis resulting from slowed processing is supported by the effects of amphetamine, which increase arousal and reduce the effects of narcosis and by the effects of alcohol that reduce arousal and increase the effects of narcosis [Hamilton, et al., 1989; Fowler, et al., 1986].

Strategic Component

Decreased accuracy on cognitive function tests with narcosis [Moeller, et al., 1981; Hesser, et al., 1978; Fothergill, et al., 1991] may be due to strategic changes in information handling attempting to compensate for slowed processing. One strategic variable is the speed-accuracy trade-off and a shift in this variable can mean that accuracy is sacrificed in an attempt to maintain the speed of responses [Fowler, et al., 1985; Hesser, et al., 1978]. Curiously, such a rapid guessing technique has been found to be typical of one population of occupational divers at the surface [Williamson, et al., 1987].

Modifying Your Dive Profile

Since inert gas narcosis is dependent on the partial pressure of the narcotic gas, it is depth dependent. As already noted some effects are more apparent at shallower depths, with other effects becoming evident deeper. The onset of narcosis upon breathing a narcotic partial pressure of gas is rapid, but not instantaneous. The time to onset of narcosis should represent the time for a narcotic tension of inert gas to be achieved in the brain, and thus can be characterized by the half time of the brain and on the depth of the dive. For typical descent rates, narcosis will onset during compression past 100 fsw (30 msw) or soon after arriving at depth. Rapid compression can temporarily raise alveolar carbon dioxide levels that can exacerbate narcosis causing a temporary higher peak level of narcosis.

Oxygen

Theoretical and experimental evidence suggests that oxygen is also narcotic, producing performance deficits similar to inert gases. Although central nervous system oxygen toxicity prevents pure oxygen breathing at a sufficiently high partial pressure to cause subjective sensations of narcosis, it can produce cognitive function impairment alone (100% O_2) or in gas mixtures containing another narcotic gas. Lipid solubility predicts oxygen could be two times as narcotic as nitrogen and cognitive function tests indicate oxygen may be three to four times as narcotic as nitrogen [Hesser, et al., 1978]. It is therefore prudent to include oxygen in any calculations of equinarcotic depths in mixed gas dive planning.

Carbon Dioxide

Carbon dioxide produces a form of narcosis that is somewhat different to inert gas narcosis, and probably involves a different mechanism [Hesser, et al., 1978;

Fothergill, et al., 1991]. Whereas inert gas narcosis decreases both speed and accuracy in cognitive function tests, carbon dioxide tends to decrease the speed only without influencing accuracy. Carbon dioxide is relatively more potent than inert gases at reducing neuromuscular coordination. Carbon dioxide is narcotic at extremely small alveolar partial pressure and can be debilitating alone or can act with inert gas narcosis. An increase in alveolar carbon dioxide from its normal level of 5.6 - 6.1 kPa to 7 - 8 kPa causes significant narcosis. Alveolar carbon dioxide can easily rise to this level due to respiratory resistance from poor equipment or the high breathing gas density of nitrogen mixtures at depth, breathing equipment dead space or inadequate pulmonary ventilation. For instance, a diver swimming at a fast sustainable pace breathing less than 15 liters/min (BTPS) may be at risk of alveolar carbon dioxide reaching narcotic levels due to inadequate alveolar ventilation.

Anxiety

Anecdotal evidence suggests that anxiety can enhance narcosis. There is some experimental evidence; greater test score decrements under open-sea conditions suggested producing anxiety in comparison to chamber tests. In one study describing the effects of narcosis in a cold open-water test at 100 fsw (30 msw), urine adrenaline and noradrenaline was elevated (a sign of stress) in those subjects showing the worst narcosis on cognitive function and dexterity tests [Davis, et al., 1972].

Arousal: Fatigue, Drugs & Alcohol

According to the slowed processing model of inert gas narcosis, any condition that influences the level of arousal will modify narcosis. Fatigue would be expected to enhance narcosis and this is the case. As previously described for amphetamine and alcohol, any drugs which produce increased or decreased arousal are likely to interact with narcosis.

Tolerance

Drug tolerance is the phenomena of reduced effect of a drug due to repeated exposure. In the context of narcosis, development of tolerance would imply a

> "Anecdotal evidence suggests that anxiety can enhance narcosis."

reduced narcotic potency of inert gas with repeated diving exposure, but this is apparently not the case since repeated diving exposure does not reduce the objective behavioral measures of inert gas narcosis. Five successive daily chamber air dives to 7 ATA each produce the same deterioration compared to 1.3 ATA in cognitive tests, reaction time and dexterity tests [Moeller et al., 1981]. Body sway (i.e. a measure of intoxication) is similarly increased by narcosis at 5.5 ATA compared to 1.3 ATA over 12 successive daily air dives. [Rogers and Moeller, 1989] Clearly, tolerance to the narcotic actions of inert gases does not develop; repetitive diving exposures do not reduce the anesthetic potency of inert gases.

Subjective Adaptation

Adaptation is the adjustment by an organism to its environment; in the case of narcosis, adaptation would be a rearrangement of behavior that allows a performance enhancement. Repeated diving produces a dissociation of behavioral and subjective components of narcosis. It is unclear whether this represents a true tolerance or an adaptation. During five consecutive daily dives to 6.46 ATA on air, reaction time does not improve relative to 1 ATA, but subjective evaluation of narcosis does change. Global estimates of the magnitude of narcosis begin to decline by the third daily dive as does identification of body/mental sensations associated with intoxication; however, subjects continue to describe their ability to work as being equally impaired [Hamilton, et al., 1995]. It is evident that it is inappropriate to use the intensity of sensations of intoxication sensation as a gauge for underwater efficiency.

Specific Adaptation & Individual Variability

It is entrenched in the diving community that some individuals can work effectively at depth and experience improves performance during deep dives. Indeed, as with any biological phenomena, there is some individual variability in susceptibility to narcosis, but whether adaptation specific to the narcotic situation occurs with repeated exposures is speculative. Reduction in subjective sensations of intoxication may allow better focus of the task at hand. Some individuals may adopt more appropriate adaptive strategies to cope with narcosis and experience may also help identify such strategies. It is possible to control accuracy on tests for narcosis, allowing only speed to decline [Fowler, et al., 1993], so a potential strategic adaptation could be to choose an appropriate speed-accuracy trade-off. Indeed, one of the earliest observations of narcosis is that using deliberately slow movements can lessen neuromuscular impairment [Behnke, et al., 1935].

Notes:

Notes:

Summary & Practical Strategies

Some inert gases possess anesthetic properties; narcosis results from breathing these gases at sub-anesthetic doses and is an unavoidable consequence of air diving beyond 100 fsw (30 msw). A possible explanation of the effects of narcosis on behavior is a slowing of information processing in the CNS, often combined with a shift in speed and accuracy making the diver more prone to errors. The subjective sensations of inert gas narcosis include intoxication and repeated diving may reduce these sensations. Objective laboratory tests of narcosis show slow and inaccurate cognitive function, slowed reaction time, and decreased neuromuscular coordination. Performance on such tests does not improve with repeated dives. A less well-appreciated action of inert gas narcosis is impaired thermoregulation, which can result in greater heat loss during immersion. Since narcosis is enhanced by carbon dioxide retention, anxiety and fatigue, narcosis can increase during a dive without further change in depth.

Strategies to enhance performance with narcosis might exist. Although the nature of such strategies is unknown, some issues are worthy of consideration. First, recognize that narcosis will reduce efficiency during air dives deeper than 100 fsw (30 msw). Also, owing to subjective adaptation, it is inappropriate to use the intensity of intoxication as a gauge for underwater safety and efficiency. Secondly, over-learned skills are less likely to be influenced by impaired information processing. Furthermore, subjective adaptation may be of some value particularly for performing over-learned tasks. On the other hand, subjective adaptation will be of no value to novel situations or situations requiring cognitive information processing or memory (i.e. gas management or deco calculations). Thirdly, if some of the performance decrement is due to an inappropriate shift in speed-accuracy trade-off, training may allow more appropriate information processing strategies to be implemented.

Finally, it must be recognized that such strategies may improve performance with moderate levels of narcosis but are unlikely to protect against the debilitating effects of extreme narcosis.

By far the best choice is to avoid narcosis where feasible and where safety may be reduced. The level of narcosis is primarily influenced by inspired partial pressures of nitrogen and oxygen, in other words depth and breathing gas mixture. The use of helium as a partial or complete replacement for nitrogen as a breathing gas diluent reduces or eliminates inert gas narcosis and owing to lower breathing gas density reduces the level of narcosis due to carbon dioxide build-up.

We are assuming that most divers are quite familiar with decompression sickness (DCS); therefore I will skip the background information. However, to really understand and appreciate DCS risk factors, you must understand the 'pathophysiology' of DCS. We find it useful to think of DCS as a 'stress/sickness' continuum. When there is no dive, there is no stress. A short and shallow dive produces some stress on the body due to the additional dissolved inert gas, but there are no symptoms. A deeper and longer dive can result in mild signs or symptoms due to the higher gas load, directly or indirectly. These symptoms do not require treatment, do not result in any permanent damage, and are called 'decompression stress.' Examples of decompression stress include skin itch, mildly red areas of skin without pain or swelling, 'niggles' (i.e. fleeting pains of joints and muscles), and fatigue disproportionate to the situation that

> ## "Any factor that increases the amount inert gas in the body at the end of the dive is going to increase the risk of DCS."

is often associated with large numbers of intravascular bubbles. A more severe dive might result in symptoms that will result in mild permanent damage if they are not treated. We call this mild decompression sickness (i.e. skin bends, lymphatic bends, mild pain, historically called DCS Type I). An even longer and deeper dive might result in severe symptoms with serious damage, even if treated. We would call this serious decompression sickness or Central nervous system (CNS), spinal cord, pulmonary, and/or inner ear decompression sickness, which is historically called DCS Type II. The end of the scale is death resulting from decompression sickness. This is extremely rare today but still occasionally happens when someone omits the equivalent of several hours of required decompression.

The first underlying principle is that the more inert gas in the body at the end of the dive, the higher the risk of DCS. Therefore, any factor that increases the amount inert gas in the body at the end of the dive is going to increase the risk of DCS. There are several secondary factors and we will look at them as they come up.

Inert gas uptake and elimination can be seen as either 'diffusion' or 'perfusion' limited. We believe the vast majority of blood that passes through the lung capillaries equilibrates with the gas in the alveoli (oxygen and carbon-dioxide equilibrate, so why shouldn't inert gas) and also equilibrates with the tissues when it passes through the tissue capillaries. Therefore, inert gas uptake and elimination are primarily determined by blood flow (i.e. perfusion limited).

Pathophysiology is the detailed changes that occur in the body in disease. In DCS, the pathophysiology is only partially understood, and what we do understand is quite complex. There seem to be several different 'disease processes', all of which we call DCS.

Different Types of Decompression Sickness (DCS)

The most common form of DCS presents with pain as the only symptom (roughly 80% of cases when the divers are closely supervised and there is no 'cost' to being bent, i.e. most cases will be reported). The pain is generally in or around a joint but can be anywhere, even in a muscle belly. It ranges from mild to unbearable, tends to be steady, deep and boring in nature; it may be increased by movement, or relieved by local pressure. The nature of the pain is 'different' and if the person has been bent before, they will recognize the nature of the pain. The cause of the pain is unknown. There are lots of theories. One theory is that bubbles are causing elevated pressure in the bone marrow resulting in ischemia of bone and thus pain. Somehow the complement system also has to be involved but more about that later.

Lymphatic Bends

Lymphatic bends are easy to understand. Bubbles form in the lymphatic vessels and move up the lymphatic tree until they are trapped in the lymph nodes. The injured person has swollen, tender lymph nodes and the skin in the area drained by the involved lymphatic is swollen and indurated, meaning pitting edema. It is not usually painful. This will resolve without treatment, probably without significant damage, but treatment speeds resolution.

Skin Bends

Skin bends are also fairly straightforward, although there is a lot of debate in this area. The involved area of skin is swollen, painful, and has blotchy discoloration described as mottling or marbling. If left alone, it will resolve over several days, again most likely without significant permanent damage but treatment results in rapid resolution. The problem is most likely obstruction of blood vessels in the skin by bubbles. Some believe it is due to brain damage, but that is speculation.

CNS or Brain Bends

CNS or brain bends are complex. Multiple sites of injury in the brain mean that almost any imaginable sign or symptom is possible. Serious permanent damage is highly likely if these individuals are not treated and even with treatment, residual problems are common. The exact pathophysiology is still being debated. One theory, especially in altitude bends, is that bubbles form in the fatty tissues of the brain. When saturated, fat will contain approximately five times more nitrogen then water. The brain contains large amounts of fat. Ascending to altitude is decompressing from saturation and therefore, fat will contain large amounts of excess nitrogen. CNS symptoms are relatively common in altitude bends and less common in diving DCS. This is to be expected, as fat tends to have a relatively poor blood supply and therefore takes up nitrogen slowly during a single scuba dive. A second theory in CNS signs and symptoms is bubbles that have crossed over from the venous blood, essentially causing arterial gas embolism.

Spinal Cord Bends

With spinal cord bends, the person presents weakness or total paralysis and reduced or absent sensation in the legs. They often cannot urinate but move their bowels without control. Low back and abdominal pain are often present. The circulation of the spine is unique in that the blood goes from the capillaries into a network of small veins, all the same size (the capillaries in the rest of the body drain into veins that get progressively larger). Animal research has shown that bubbles collect and get stuck in these 'venous networks' and obstruct the circulation, thereby depriving a section of the spinal cord of oxygen and nutrients. Treatment as soon as possible is obviously required.

Pulmonary DCS

Pulmonary DCS or 'chokes' is due to obstruction of the circulation through the lungs by bubbles. When a person has a large excess of inert gas in the body, it tends to come out of solution in the small veins and get carried back to the heart and then to the lungs where it is trapped because the bubbles are too large to be pushed through the capillaries. This is not a problem for the vast majority of people because at rest, all of the blood being pumped by the heart goes through only 10% of the capillaries in the lungs. Therefore, if we obstruct 10% of the lung capillaries, another 10% will open and take the blood flow. The trapped bubbles will slowly off gas into the alveoli and disappear in approximately 45 minutes. The person is completely unaware of this process until over 90% of the lung capillaries are obstructed. Then, the pressure in the pulmonary arteries rise, the lungs fill up with fluid, and the person has great difficulty breathing. The heart can not pump enough blood through the obstructed lungs, the person goes into shock, and usually dies. The important question is, "how many bubbles are required to cause this problem?" In 1929, Clark injected air into a peripheral vein of a dog at a rate of 50 ml per minute until he had injected a total of 2.0 liters of air into the dog. The dog could not have cared less. Therefore, we know that 'several liters' of gas are required to cause pulmonary DCS. The only way to get this many bubbles is to omit several hours of decompression. Therefore, pulmonary DCS is seldom a problem in scuba diving.

Inner Ear DCS

Inner ear DCS (vestibular) is due to the formation of bubbles in the inner ear. The bubbles most likely disrupt the membrane between the endo and peri lymph, allowing them to mix. The person notices a sudden onset of severe vertigo, tinnitus, nausea, vomiting, and hearing loss. Inner ear DCS is rare and usually associated with

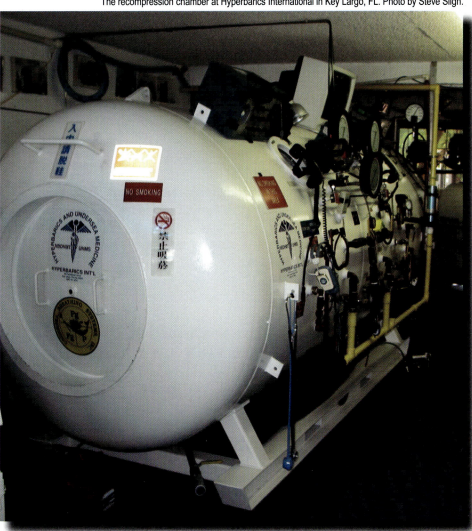

The recompression chamber at Hyperbarics International in Key Largo, FL. Photo by Steve Sligh.

gas switches at depth. It responds poorly to treatment and should not be a problem for most technical divers. The bubbles are thought to form because of 'Inert Gas Counterdiffusion' and this has been observed even when the divers do not change depth. Further discussion of this problem is beyond the scope of this manual.

Bubble Trouble

So what can we say in general about the pathophysiology of DCS? Bubbles seem to be a necessary 'first step'. Nearly all cases of DCS where the diver has had good Doppler monitoring showed large numbers of intravascular bubbles. However, only 5-10% of divers with large numbers of intravascular bubbles develop signs or symptoms of DCS.

In some forms of DCS, the bubbles are a direct cause of the symptoms by causing vascular obstruction (pulmonary and spinal DCS). Bubbles are highly unlikely to ever form in arteries, as the pressure in arteries is approximately 100 mmHg higher than the pressure anywhere else in the body. More importantly, the blood in arteries (excluding the pulmonary artery which contains venous blood) has just come from the lungs where it off loaded the excess inert gas and therefore, arterial blood does not contain the excess inert gas required to form bubbles. If however, bubbles can bypass the pulmonary filter (i.e. the lungs) and go directly from the veins to the arteries, we get arterial gas bubbles and CNS signs and symptoms. This is probable in PFO (large, patent, foramen ovale - a hole in the heart) but also possible in other situations. This seems to be an important but relatively rare cause of problems in divers. Never-the-less, any diver who undertakes dives where they have a reasonable risk of developing large numbers of intravascular bubbles (a hard question to answer but a concern when doing dives requiring more than 30 minutes of decompression) should be checked to determine if they have an open foramen ovale (echocardiogram with bubble contrast injected into a peripheral vein, repeated with a valsalva maneuver).

Intravascular bubbles may only be a marker of significant excess inert gas. Bubbles forming in tissues may cause signs and symptoms by tissue distortion. This is quite likely in altitude CNS bends. It is also probable in inner ear DCS. Some people believe that tissue bubbles cause the pain in 'pain only' bends by pressing on nerves or tendons. These bubbles have never been demonstrated, even after extensive attempts, so I think other explanations are more likely (e.g. raised intramedullary pressure).

Another way in which intravascular bubbles might cause the signs and symptoms of DCS is by interaction with other elements in blood. The body attacks the bubbles. Platelets are used up, red blood cells stick together, white blood cells are activated, and sometimes the complement system is activated. Research at DCIEM and the University of Toronto suggests that activation of the complement system is a necessary 'second step' in DCS. Only animals that have large numbers of intravascular bubbles and a complement system that is activated by those bubbles, on that particular day, go on to develop the signs or symptoms of DCS. Some human testing also shows similar results. Therefore, for the most common forms of DCS, we seem to need a large inert gas load as reflected by large numbers of intravascular bubbles, and a complement system that is activated

The barber shop on the USS Saratoga. Photo by Fabio Amaral.

by those bubbles before we will develop the signs or symptoms of DCS. DCS can actually be thought of as an immune/inflammatory response.

Risk Factors

Now, let's look at each of the risk factors for DCS and explore how their effects are revealed. Let's also look at how we can reduce our risk of DCS on all dives.

A relatively large number of factors have been observed to increase the risk of DCS. For a given dive profile, the less decompression you do, the higher the risk of DCS. It's simple. Less off gassing during decompression so more inert gas left in the body at the end of the dive. As an aside, a short stop, deeper than your first required decompression stop, to reduce the likelihood of bubbles forming during decompression makes sense. Using decompression gas with less inert gas (nitrox or pure oxygen) also is preferable, as more inert gas will be eliminated during each minute of the decompression stop.

"If you get cold during decompression, you should do more decompression to avoid getting bent!"

Exercising Before Diving

Heavy exercise before diving results in an elevated heart rate for several hours (increased inert gas uptake during the dive). It also might generate large numbers of micronuclei (increased numbers of bubbles after the dive). Heavy exercise might leave the diver tired and they will have to exert themselves harder during the dive than if they were well rested (elevated heart rate during the dive and increased inert gas uptake). It might result in some tissue damage (wear and tear on muscles) and thereby increase the risk of an inflammatory/immune response.

Heavy exercise during the dive results in an elevated heart rate and therefore, increased inert gas uptake (more inert gas in the body at the end of the dive). A moderate work rate (O_2 uptake of 2.0 liters per minute, easily done) during the dive triples the required amount of decompression compared to a very relaxed dive! On

A diver uses a DPV to explore a wreck. Photo by Greg Lawlor.

the same note, stress, fear, anxiety all elevate the heart rate and should have the same effect. New divers have a higher risk of DCS, as do divers who have been stressed during the dive.

Fitness Level

Fitness level has the same explanation. The more fit diver will have a lower heart rate during the dive and pump less blood through the lungs, thereby absorbing less inert gas than the less fit diver.

Experience

Experience also has the same effect. The more experienced diver should be more efficient during the dive and work less. They should also be much more relaxed and have a lower heart rate. Just to clarify, it is not really the heart rate that matters but the cardiac output (the amount of blood the heart is pumping). In general, heart rate reflects cardiac output.

Exercising After Diving

Exercise after the dive is a bit more complex. If the diver is not bubbling, exercise should have no effect. However, exercise in a bubbling diver results in a shower of bubbles and this seems to be associated with an increased risk of DCS. This shower of bubbles will expose the body to a large gas surface area and increase the likelihood of complement activation. Experience supports the importance of this risk factor. As far back at 1873 it was noted by Dr. A. Smith, one of the Brooklyn Bridge Caisson Physicians, "exercise as little as may be during the first hour after coming out and lie down if possible." The caisson workers were doing 'dives' that are now known to be very stressful and should result in large numbers of intravascular bubbles. After the first hour, the number of intravascular bubbles should have been much lower. The same advice holds today. When you do a stressful dive and have a reasonable likelihood of bubbling, take it easy for the first hour after the dive. Sit around and have lunch before you carry your doubles back to the truck.

Fatigue

Fatigue before the dive will result in a higher workload, higher heart rate and more inert gas uptake during the dive. Getting cold during decompression will reduce the flow of blood to the arms and legs. Therefore, less inert gas will be removed during decompression and the diver will have more inert gas in the body at the end of

Notes:

the dive. Therefore, if you get cold during decompression, you should do more decompression to avoid getting bent!

Dehydration

Dehydration is a major risk factor. All divers become dehydrated during the dive for many different reasons including immersion diuresis, cold diuresis, dry breathing gas, sweating, etc. Some divers intentionally dehydrate themselves before the dive so that they will not have to urinate in their wet or dry suit. A dehydrated diver will have less circulating blood volume and will off-gas less efficiently, therefore, having more inert gas in the body at the end of the dive. Therefore, drink plenty of fluids before the dive; electrolyte solutions like Gatorade are recommended as more water stays in the body and less urine is produced during the dive.

Illness

Illness is a contributor. Any diver who is 'sick' with an infection has an increased risk of DCS. They will usually be tired, have an elevated heart rate, are often dehydrated, and have a complement system that has been 'primed' to be activated by bubbles. According to unpublished observation on the DCIEM data, smokers are more likely to bubble than non-smokers. This might be due to the chemical changes in the body caused by smoking, the lung damage caused by smoking, or it might reflect a lower level of fitness in smokers.

Medications & Drugs

Medications and drugs will increase, reduce, or have no effect on the risk of DCS. Any drug that increases the heart rate should increase the risk of DCS. Any drug that stimulates the CNS should increase your risk of oxygen toxicity. Any drug that depresses the CNS should increase the level of inert gas narcosis. For most drugs, their effect on DCS risk is unknown.

Obesity

Obesity is difficult to evaluate. The fat will not be a significant source of inert gas during a single bounce dive but might become important in a series of stressful dives or in altitude DCS. Obese people tend to have a lower level of physical fitness and that will increase their

"Any diver who is 'sick' with an infection has an increased risk of DCS."

risk of DCS. Conversely, the obese diver will tend to stay warmer during decompression, thereby reducing their risk of DCS. The ideal cold water diver has a bit of excess weight but maintains a high level of physical fitness.

Pre-Existing Significant Injury

A pre-existing significant injury will increase the risk of DCS in the area of the injury for many years. This is most likely a result of scar tissue and altered blood flow in that area. If you are bent, treated with complete resolution of symptoms and then bent again within the next several months, you will almost certainly be bent in the same area. If you experienced complete relief during the treatment, then the tissues are still damaged and the blood flow is altered. This will take months or years to heal.

Age

Age is a factor. Older divers have a higher risk of DCS than younger divers. Older divers tend to be less fit than younger divers. Older divers tend to have too much, or too little body fat. But older divers are often more relaxed and efficient. Older divers also tend to do less stressful dives and/or be more 'smart' about their diving. Like mild obesity, age is a very complex risk factor.

Diving and Flying

Ascending to altitude or flying after diving will increase your risk of DCS by increasing the amount of 'excess' inert gas in the body. The amount of inert gas in the body does not change when you ascend to altitude, but the amount of inert gas required for the tissues to be saturated 'decreases' with altitude. Thereby leaving you with more 'excess' inert gas in the body.

In aviation DCS, women, on average, seem about twice as likely to get bent as men. The risk varies with the menstrual cycle, being 4 times higher during menses and equivalent just before (averaging twice the rate for men). The data for diving is not good enough to detect such a small difference but there is no reason to believe diving DCS should be any different than altitude DCS, in this area. This topic is complicated by the fact that women tend to have more body fat, smaller mass, and larger relative surface area (i.e. get cold easier) when compared to men. However, if women do have an increased risk of DCS in diving, it has little practical significance (i.e. the other risk factors are much more important).

Acclimatization

Finally, does a series of 'work-up' or 'acclimatization' dives reduce your risk of DCS?

Research done at DCIEM to try to address this question gave equivocal results. For most people, work-up dives reduced the sensitivity of their complement system to activation by bubbles. However, for some individuals, their complement system was 'sensitized' to activation by bubbles. Therefore, it would seem that most individuals actually do have a reduced risk of DCS after a series of work-up dives but there is no way to tell whether the risk is rising or falling in a particular individual. Also, a series of dives always has the possibility of buildup of residual inert gas in slow tissues. The primary advantage of work-up dives before a major dive is that the diver will be more relaxed and comfortable during the 'big dive.' An added benefit is you also ensure your equipment works properly!

"In aviation, women, on average, seem about twice as likely to get bent as men."

Summary

We need to ensure that we are well rested and well hydrated before every dive. Avoid smoking and all drugs. Attain and maintain a high level of physical fitness. Strive to be an efficient, calm, stress free diver with well-adjusted equipment. This requires that you dive regularly, and progress slowly when you expand your diving into a new dimension. When things go wrong, as they inevitably will, remember this discussion and adjust your dive plan to take into account your risk factors. One simple approach for divers who have a higher risk (over 40 and not a world class athlete) is to dive Nitrox 32 or 36 and decompress as if you were diving air. Your risk of DCS becomes extremely small. Be realistic about your limitations. Change those things you can change, and learn to take the rest into consideration when you plan your dives.

Each time man ventures forth to explore new environments, he encounters new physical and mental challenges and faces new hazards. In order to cope with and overcome, he must adapt and learn new behaviors. This chapter will discuss some of the adaptation, behavioral modification and conditioning that relates to the specific challenges and demands of diving.

Advances in scuba technology and planning have allowed divers to reach unthinkable depths and underwater durations. But, there is a price to be paid. As divers go deeper and travel greater distances, they must be prepared to face the hazards and challenges that accompany these extended limits.

Today's exploratory dives push and often exceed the comfort level of even the most experienced and hardened diver. Overcoming the physical and mental challenges of such dives is a matter of behavior modification – a process that requires the diver to develop a unity of the mind, body, and spirit.

Many factors influence the way a diver reacts to the demands and hazards of their environment. These factors include attitude, awareness, physical fitness, self-discipline and his ability to separate perceptions from reality. To understand this phenomenon, examine the various mental and physical stimuli that influence a diver's attitude and performance.

Stress in Deeper Diving

Stress plays a major role in our actions and reactions. Underwater, reacting to stress is the difference between an enjoyable dive and an accident. Stress is a phenomenon that may, if unchecked, lead to panic and result in an accident. Technical divers are exposed to most known stresses measured by psychologists.

Wrecks and caves present us with an overhead environment. This means we cannot escape directly to the surface as we do in no-decompression stop open water diving. Caves and wrecks are dark. They usually present us with "tough" choices. Deciding which passage or companionway to take in a seemingly endless maze can create its own stress. As we review each stress source, it will become apparent how these environmental hazards add up.

Time-pressure stress is present in many scenarios. Simply, time-pressure stress involves matching the gas supply to dive duration. This expands into a major problem when a dive plan has been exceeded and the gas supply

is low. Uninformed or unskilled divers may actually compound the problem by increasing their breathing rates. Time-pressure can also build when a diver looks at their decompression "clock."

Distance presents a major time-pressure stress. The greater the distance to open water, the more time stress has to build. The greater danger in distance-related stress is the perceived time-pressure threat. In this case, the perception is usually greater than the actual threat. There have been numerous instances when divers have become so distressed they forgot basic and important rules for diving.

Preparing for a dive can also cause time-pressure stress. For example, if one diver has entered the water and their buddy has an equipment problem and removes gear to make repairs. Time stresses both divers – the one who has to wait and the one causing the delay because they have to play catch up. Confinement is obviously stressful. This is usually lurking in the recesses of the mind and comes into play when other stresses are introduced. Confinement adds time-pressure stress with distance. The "knee jerk" reaction to bolt toward the surface must be overcome by overhead training that discourages thinking about the traditional escape route. In this way, confinement stress is managed.

> "Underwater, reacting to stress is the difference between an enjoyable dive and an accident."

Task loading stress occurs when divers perform more tasks than they feel they can handle. Task loading can happen when a diver is trying to do three simple things at once – manage a reel, two cylinders and swim correctly, while staying relaxed. Add a Diver Propulsion Vehicle (DPV) or other specialized items, and the diver's ability to function may be impaired. With experience, divers learn to handle multiple tasks with greater ease, but each time an additional action or responsibility is added, stress will increase.

Incorrect breathing patterns are tied to stress. Incorrect breathing creates stress, but stress will cause incorrect breathing and compound the diver's condition. Once this pattern begins, a vicious cycle develops. The pattern is often so subtle a diver may not even recognize it. Examples of stressful breathing include hyperventilation and rapid breathing. Both result in a feeling of air starvation. This is frequently confused for regulator failure. A diver who fails to exhale and keeps inhaling in small "gulps" until their lungs are full often suspects a faulty regulator.

To break this cycle, a diver must be aware of and regain breathing control. Divers should practice diaphragm breathing and concentrate on slow, deep breaths until it becomes a reflex. When a diver first feels stress or discomfort, it's important for them to stop all activity, exhale slowly, and then inhale slowly and completely. This breathing pattern should be repeated at least three

faster than others. Exceeding our "hull speed" takes more work and produces a minimal increase in performance. Unwanted respiratory induced stress will result.

Unlike boats, divers can change the shape of their "hulls". A lean profile produces less drag and is more efficient. Divers should maintain a lean personal profile through exercise and proper diet, but a lean profile also involves the diver's swim posture and equipment configuration.

Billy Deans pratices a black-out drill. Photo courtesy of Billy Deans.

Poor swim posture may lead to stress and requires more energy to maintain. This increased energy demand, and in turn, makes increased demands on our respiratory system.

Exertion and thermal imbalance produce stress, if the diver is either too hot or too cold. An aware diver should be able to control these stressors simply by monitoring comfort level and using adequate and appropriate thermal protection.

Ego threats, or peer pressure, are indirect sources of stress, particularly if they cause a diver to attempt feats beyond their own personal ability or comfort level.

Disorientation is always a problem when exploring overhead environments or deep water.

Wrecks are exciting, but require more planning to penetrate safely. Photo of Patti Mount, by Tom Mount.

times before resuming the dive. The diver should then continue breathing slowly using the diaphragm muscles. Discomfort can almost always be alleviated by this method.

A good way to avoid breathing stress is developing a swim pace that allows acceptable forward momentum while maintaining a correct, comfortable respiratory pattern. Accelerating one's swimming stroke will frequently lead to uncontrolled breathing and can produce uneasiness.

Divers who maintain good physical conditioning will discover the body is like a boat hull. Once a boat reaches "hull speed," doubling the power produces little or no increase in forward momentum. Divers bodies behave similarly. Bodies, like hulls, come in different shapes. Some shapes pass through the water easier and

Most overhead environments feature multiple passages. Deep water allows little time for correction of navigational errors. Both environments create the possibility of becoming lost. The proper use of navigational tools such as visual referencing, compasses, line arrows and guidelines can offset the stress of disorientation and the risk of becoming lost. One of the leading causes of deaths in overhead environment dives is the failure to follow a continuous guideline.

Darkness or loss of visibility produces sensory-loss stress. This can be a result of a light malfunction, low visibility, turbid water or silt outs. While this should not be a major concern in and of itself, when combined with other stresses and performance inhibitors, loss of visibility can lead to threatening situations.

Notes:

common behavioral modifications that can result in "mental narrowing," or more aptly stated, becoming unfocused as it relates to problem solving. By becoming overly focused, the diver may lose the ability to correctly analyze situations and to perform both newly learned and well-known skills. Mental narrowing can compound the problem because of falsely perceived task loading. This type of behavioral change, if not corrected, may lead to panic.

The body's physical reactions to the psychological trauma of stress may include increased respiration, increased heart rate, abnormal adrenaline release, and the instinctive flight response.

For survival, it is imperative that we compensate for behavioral and physiological change. Tools that help control stress include awareness, adequate training and the application of newly acquired skills. In addition, we must develop a new discipline or attitude. We must be able to instantly recognize a real threat as opposed to a perceived one, and we must instinctively make the appropriate corrective action in order to avoid disaster.

Awareness is developed through a process of self and group analysis. Awareness must become automatic. One of the best ways to accomplish this is employing the process of mental visualization prior to the actual dive. Running the dive in your mind beforehand can result in a safer dive. Awareness also opens the mind's ability to detect changes in dive performance that otherwise would go unnoticed in yourself or your dive companions. During the dive periodically ask yourself, "Am I comfortable? Is everything really OK?" Observe buddies and their comfort levels and listen for changes in respiratory rates.

The need for intensive, repetitive training of all pertinent skills becomes apparent when a situation takes a critical turn. Poorly learned skills will be forgotten in times of duress. Only skills that were practiced until virtually instinctive will remain with the diver.

The first step in any stress control and behavior modification program should be a personal training program. Personal training needs to be ongoing; it is the key to maintaining a record of safe diving. To do this, continue to practice relevant skills. As part of this of this exercise, practice efficient breathing. Continually evaluate and configure dive equipment so it's easy to use, every element is accessible and it works dependably. Routinely review your skills, and as your interests expand seek additional training. Select dive buddies who share your interests and training objectives.

Risk Management

Effective risk management is the key to good technical diving. Risk management helps divers learn to

Stress can also include buoyancy problems, excessive dependency on another diver, and real or perceived physical threats. Early recognition of the telltale signs and symptoms of stress can help reduce or prevent the escalation of the stress reaction. Personal indicators of stress often include an uneasy feeling, unusual anxiety, apprehension or irritability. Our intuitive hunches will attempt to tell us if there is a reason for stress. Becoming tuned in to our inner-self is an important part of stress-free diving. Developing such a degree of awareness requires training and the use of mind control techniques.

Stress control can be accomplished through self-awareness. Frequently, the stressed diver is unaware of an increase in respiration. A buddy who notices that his/her dive partner is breathing quickly or unusually, should immediately alert him/her to momentarily remain at rest until the breathing problem is solved. To control stress, we must first be aware of it and then execute a corrective action. When dealing with stress remember that while its cause may be either real or perceived, the results are equally dangerous. Also keep in mind that stress frequently manifests itself by a change in respiration.

As divers, we must learn to recognize some

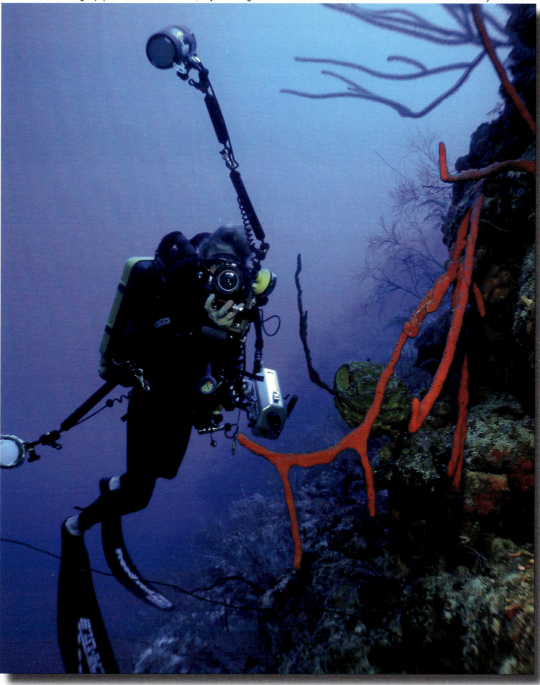
Adding equipment, such as cameras, to your configuration can create additional stress. Photo of Chris Brandson by Tom Mount.

establish realistic objectives. They can then decide what kind of diver they really want to be – a recreational diver, a technical diver or an explorer.

As we continue to emphasize, there are many risks in diving. There are also various solutions to most of the risks. Once you accept a given level of risk, you must also consider what compromises you need to make. You must weigh efficiency with safety, recognize the hazards and the benefits, and deal with the positives and the negatives.

Many various factors will enter into these compromises, including the size of the dive team, equipment configuration, capabilities, decompression risk and level of acceptable discomfort. As tech divers, we must review these factors and determine the limits of our personal comfort and control zones. Many paths will lead to the same destination in exploration or enjoyment. The quickest path often yields the greatest risk, but produces a more immediate return. The more deliberate path may take longer to arrive at the same destination, but provides greater safety. It comes down to individual risk management and how much risk you're prepared for.

Equipment configuration can provide a good illustration of the risk evaluation and management process. It allows a diver to weigh the advantages and disadvantages of a given piece of equipment, with regards to the overall safety of the dive.

For example, the more streamlined our equipment, the greater our in-water efficiency. Our gas consumption is lower, we swim easier and more efficiently, and our stamina improves. So, why not always opt for the maximum efficiency? Risk may cause some divers to configure equipment with added drag to compensate for equipment failure. For instance, one diver may dive with a single BC bladder, although BC failure may prevent the diver from surfacing. Another diver on the same dive may elect to dive with a backup BC as insurance for a safe ascent, even if it creates added drag and a slight increase in gas consumption.

Given a choice, most divers prefer a configuration that reduces drag. But, there's a chance your single bladder BC could fail and be life-threatening. It makes good sense to sacrifice being streamlined for redundancy. If doing so, divers should take into account the additional gas consumption from the increased drag and plan for this accordingly.

You need to ask yourself, "How often has your BC malfunctioned and is this a significant risk to be considered?" In the past 5 years, I have had two malfunctions, which made my BC absolutely useless for ascent. I have also witnessed other incidents of BC bladder/inflator malfunction. These incidents have convinced me that redundancy was a small price to pay for safety. If you decide to use a back up BC, ask your instructor to help you select one that offers as little drag as possible while providing adequate lift to achieve neutral buoyancy.

Additional considerations should be evaluated in a similar fashion. Some divers use two submersible pressure gauges (SPGs) on their primary gas supplies. Others feel this adds drag, and if their primary gas-supply components fail – terminate the dive. Given this choice, one SPG is enough. In fact, many feel the extra SPG is just something else to break. Those who feel redundant SPGs are necessary say that safety is the overriding issue. It all comes down to personal choice and comfort.

When configuring equipment, consideration must be given for each piece of redundant equipment. The idea of "bringing it along" must be coupled with increased drag. Thus, choose carefully. Realistically decide what produces personal safety and what is simply redundant for redundancy's sake.

There are numbers of additional topics regarding risk assessment and risk management applications. These topics could fill an entire text by themselves. Hopefully, listing a few examples is sufficient to stimulate thinking about, recognizing and evaluating what risks might really be encountered during a given dive.

Opt for a level of risk you can live with. The best determination is one that allows you control over your own destiny – worded another way, a profile that acknowledges, "Only you can breathe for you, swim for you or think for you." A dive plan determined survivable by you is a matter of personal choice.

If this is your first or thousandth dive, approach risk management the same way regardless. The first step is to list all the anticipated risk associated with the dive. Then, define how each risk affects safety. Second, prepare a plan of action to cope with stresses on the dive. Third, determine which risks are acceptable to you. Fourth, outline your equipment needs (for accomplishment and personal safety). Last, develop an operational plan providing a set of limits that make you comfortable.

Regardless of what you decide, expect others to probably challenge your decisions. The debate of risk management vs. efficiency is an eternal one. There are minimums all should agree on, but the specifics are totally individual.

Diver Capability

Herein lays the critical point in being a safe diver. There are many issues that contribute to this and offer increased performance. Life support systems, equipment configuration, equipment reducing failure points, all enhance performance but it is the raw capability of the diver that will determine the safety foundation.

To discuss diver capability, definitions must be established. Capability is having ability or competence. It includes qualities that may be used or developed, thus one's potential can be determined. To have or develop capability requires a combination of awareness of the environment, skillful efficient swimming, and detailed diving techniques, evolving to a good body attitude and practicing. Experience is valuable to diver capability. Experience also contributes through continued use of correct skills and techniques. However, experience may also be a negative influence if the diver's early experience did not lay a firm foundation in basics skills, techniques, attitudes and risk awareness. If one routinely practices a bad technique, then this bad technique is "perfected" and becomes a stumbling block for growth as a diver.

Diver capability begins in the first open water class and evolves through continuing education, practical application and knowledge. It is therefore important that the initial training be strict. Unfortunately, many dive instructors, even instructor trainers and course directors do not have a good foundation in dive technique. It is quite common in advanced and technical training to re-

"When configuring equipment, consideration must be given for each piece of redundant equipment."

teach highly "experienced" instructors the correct way to kick or achieve proper body attitude. In many cases these persons have "perfected" a bad technique, sometimes accompanied by the attitude, "because I'm an instructor, I can do no wrong." In these cases technique has to be developed, old habits broken, and also the attitude must be altered. In most sports, optimum performance comes from mastering techniques, and then "going for it." Technique is everything. I also teach martial arts and one of the most difficult things to tell people is to relax, breathe out as they strike or prepare to get hit, and develop proper technique.

The same is true in diving: relaxed and correct breathing combined with relaxed muscles when executing correct form and even calculated movements is how performance is improved. For instance, on a kick, ensuring the toes are pointed in a relaxed manner makes a world a difference in power on a flutter kick. With a frog kick, technique is the difference between being almost useless and having a strong, efficient tool. During this kick, being relaxed as the legs spread out and then cupping the toes followed by an inward thrust that brings the toes together is very important. If one is flexible enough, this thrusting before the heels touch provides the majority of forward momentum. When a diver does not bring the fins together, they are quite inefficient in realizing the full potential of this technique. Learning ascent techniques, especially in dry suits, also adds to diver capability.

Thus, the primary goal at all levels of diver education is to increase the diver's capability in the environments that they are trained in. The secondary goals will include equipment selection and configuration that will enhance performance. But, remember these will be wasted if a capable diver is not using them.

One instructor overhead two technical instructors discuss the most important aspects of a technical course. The least experienced instructor was trying to explain how the most important thing was equipment configuration. The 20-year veteran instructor just smiled and then started listing the entire component that a technical diver had to master, such as stress management, body posture and advanced skills. The list continued for about five minutes. At the end, the new instructor conceded that capability was the number one objective followed by increased performance. He agreed that configuration, although quite important, is included in the increased performance category rather than the primary goal of a training program.

A capable diver, once efficient in technique, must also become capable of managing stress. Diving is an activity that removes us from our natural habitat. You must anticipate that a stressful event will occur at some

point, someday on some dive. A diver trained in stress management will not yield to stress but will automatically respond with a corrective measure. To ensure this type of response, the diver must be exposed to simulated reality-based situations during training. The most serious are gas failure problems. Other areas include equipment failure and most importantly, behavioral failure. *IANTD programs emphasize these areas as we feel diver capability is the single most important aspect of diver safety.*

A capable diver has a foundation in good diving techniques and skills. They continue training in formal programs or by self-improvement. The capable diver employs a good attitude and has confidence. This individual defines a personal safety envelope of limits, establishes goals and directions. Once capable, this person reaches out to find avenues to increase performance, thus extending accomplishments while still maintaining a safety envelope.

Several years ago, former Vice President Dan Quayle was asked to speak at the Alliance of Black Colleges and Universities. Being one who often got things mixed up, he said with all honesty and sincerity, "It's a terrible thing to lose one's mind." What he should have said was, "A mind is a terrible thing to waste."

Seriously, our minds are the most powerful tool we possess. Scientists believe the power of the mind may be infinite. They say most of us use less than five percent of our brain's potential. Imagine for a moment what you might accomplish if you could suddenly tap into your brain's total potential.

Thoughts direct our conscious mind; we are what we think. Each and every one of us is a product of our thoughts. Our happiness, our success and our health are all influenced by what we think. These thought patterns have been embedded in our minds from the moment we began to think. They were shaped by our upbringing, past experiences and education. If we want to improve ourselves, the first step is to improve our outlook and our beliefs and thoughts.

"Thoughts direct our conscious mind; we are what we think."

By controlling our minds, we have the potential to improve our lives. Does this sound simple? It is. However, few of us have developed the discipline to think strategically. It appears most people seem to merely respond to their environment. Being ahead of the game, people with foresight and judgment shape their world. Yet, developing mental discipline and the ability to think strategically takes time. It requires you to exercise your mind. The mental exercise techniques I use include meditation, affirmations, goal setting, breathing exercises and concentration.

A physically conditioned body is necessary for creating a healthy mind. For the body to experience outstanding health, the mind must remain healthy. The mind, body and spirit all work in unison. We are, indeed, what we think. In time, we can probably make our life what we want it to be by using mind control. Some people have called it the 'right stuff'. Perhaps it is. Having the right stuff means having increased self-confidence. It means being able to accomplish important goals. Moreover, it means being able to survive when mentally and physically challenged.

Even before you being technical diving, you must prepare your mind. You must tell yourself, "I'm going in. I'm going to do everything right. And, I'm coming back. There's nothing in there I can't handle. I've done my homework thoroughly." This is important, because your mind must be conditioned to adjust to environmental changes once you enter a dive.

There are numerous facets to be considered. It is often necessary to overcome ingrained, negative beliefs. Self-confidence is a major component in making the right decision, especially when faced with unforeseen adverse situations. A positive self-image and self-confidence go hand-in-hand.

Often in our society, people are "brainwashed" more by what they can't accomplish rather than by what they can achieve. Many people live their lives in fear. They fear the unknown. They're afraid to leave their homes at night. All of these are negative thoughts. When you were younger, how often did someone say you couldn't do such and such, or that you were a bad person?

These statements were directed at us during our formative years and became embedded in our minds. Over time, this conditioning evolved into a belief system. To produce a positive belief system, it is often necessary to recondition our inner beliefs.

As we've said, when it comes to becoming a good technical diver, we must develop an "I can" belief system. We must program our minds. We can accomplish this with techniques of visualization and affirmation.

These powerful mechanisms change and improve belief systems. They also provide the most clear cut approach for helping us to accomplish all our desired diving goals. As stated by Henry Ford, "If you think you can, or think you can't, either way you are right."

As stated in the Bible, "Whatever a man thinketh,

so he is." Our total being is a reflection of what we think we are. Our thoughts are our reality.

Visualization is an excellent tool for developing mental control and changing beliefs. The process is quite simple. Close your eyes and concentrate on breathing slowly and deeply. You are going to slowly relax every muscle in your body. You will begin with your feet. Once these muscles feel relaxed, you'll move to the calves of your legs. Then, move slowly upward relaxing each muscle group from your big toe to the top of your head. As soon as you feel totally relaxed, form an image in your mind. This image may involve the performance of a given skill or the completion of a goal. These are the first steps to becoming your own master.

Most champion athletes and successful business people use visualization to manage their lives. It is merely a part of their total training program. If you to achieve grater success, we strongly recommended you begin a program of mental conditioning, if you aren't already doing so.

To visualize an upcoming dive, use this relaxation and visualization technique. Picture in your mind the entire dive from beginning to end. Include all dive team members. Visualize what you might see as well as what challenges you may face. Be thorough. Do the dive step by step in your mind. Once this dive has been mentally rehearsed, it's easy for your body to duplicate this performance.

When you are in a relaxed state, it's easy to communicate with your subconscious mind. If your mind "tells you" something can go wrong during your upcoming dive, sort it out. Talk to your buddies. Tell them, about your concerns. Go back and run the dive through your mind again. If you still get "bad vibes", bail out. If you're the team leader, cancel the dive.

There are numerous self-help tapes available to guide you to learn the technique of visualization. They include, for example, self-image improvement, correct breathing, goal setting, and increased concentration. While tapes are excellent materials to help you get started, eventually you'll need to customize your training to include your specific needs. No tapes are available to help you visualize an upcoming dive. The tapes will show you how to do the visualization, but after that, you're on your own.

Your pre-dive visualization can be as brief as three minutes or up to half-hour. The more serious the dive profile, the greater the detailed you should devote to the visualization. I visualize all my dives. When possible, I try to do one meditation session daily. I usually average about three meditation sessions weekly, plus pre-dive visualizations.

Notes:

Once you incorporate a meditation program into your lifestyle, you'll find yourself becoming more relaxed and able to handle stress more quickly and easily. You should also see immediate improvements in your dive performance. When diving, you should feel more relaxed and have a greater sense of confidence. Gradually, you'll discover not only your lifestyle has changed, but your entire belief system has changed as well.

When you begin the process of visualization, be patient. Negative feelings, or a sense of inadequacy, which have been a part of your life for years, cannot be

Melanie Paul practices pre-dive visualization to mentally prepare for dives. Photo by Sara Clarkin.

able to reach new levels of excellence and control.

Affirmation is the concept of stating something as if it has already happened. It is another means of communication with the subconscious mind. Affirmation can be spoken, written, or repeated during the process of visualization. A great deal of research on the effective use of affirmations has been performed in recent years. Psychiatrists, psychologists and social workers, as well as self-improvement programs are now using the results of this research. All of these are using the findings of this research to successfully help patients establish realistic goals and belief systems.

Verbal affirmations are quick, beneficial, and efficient. They play role in helping you re-program your mind. Written affirmations are more effective than verbal ones. Writing down what you want to accomplish is the best way to reach your brain's subconscious realm. Any time is good for affirmations, but many researchers conclude that the best time is 30 minutes prior to falling asleep.

It's good idea to keep a ledger to log your affirmations. The best way to do this is to divide your log into three sections. First,

changed overnight. Improvements will come gradually. Before you laugh or dismiss this idea, remember the process does work. I use it, as do most of my friends and dive buddies.

Visualization enables you to increase your self-confidence. It permits you to see yourself as you really are. Being honest with yourself is very important, not only with your abilities as a diver, but in your life as well. It is excellent for expanding awareness and for becoming more intuitive. It enables us to get to know our own selves. For the serious diver, visualization is an essential part of the dive planning process. This is the means by which you can go within yourself and make a major life commitment. Importantly, it is in these moments when we discover our real feelings about life's meaning. When this energy is channeled toward dive planning, we are

set personal goals. Second, each night write down the steps you have made to accomplish each goal. Third, log the affirmations reflecting accomplishment of an individual goal. Stating an affirmation while visualizing it is probably the best way to create an accurate personal goal or objective.

The right attitudes cause us to be responsible and expectant. We expect our actions to produce pleasant experiences. Our attitudes cause us to receive what we expect. Attitudes reflect our "inner person." Success in diving, or in business, is simply a reflection of our attitudes. Luck happens when preparedness meets opportunity. A positive attitude causes good luck. A person with a winning attitude expects and achieves success. Winning attitudes don't just happen. We create them. Remind yourself daily to continue to develop and sustain a good, positive attitude.

As our attitudes develop, we begin to learn more about ourselves. We become honest with ourselves and we begin to believe in ourselves. As this belief strengthens, self-discipline is easier. As our attitudes develop, our ability to know ourselves becomes a natural outcropping. Being true to oneself becomes a reflex. A winning attitude helps us deal favorably with stress. Most importantly, it helps us conquer the impossible!

A winning attitude causes life's energy to flow positively. As divers, we can accomplish more. As individuals, we become happier. Five statements summed up by Earl Nightingale, renowned motivator, best explains the role of attitude: "When it comes down to it, all life is just a matter of thoughts and beliefs; we are simply acting out our thoughts. The mind is capable of achieving everything it can conceive and believe. Realistic beliefs originate from thought and are improved by exercise. In the process, some minor goals evolve providing a path to achievement of major goals. Overall, long term goals are ultimately accomplished."

All the world's major philosophies and doctrines share fundamental beliefs. The Christian Bible says, "Whatsoever you ask for, ask for believing and you will receive it." If you ask with disbelief or doubt, it is unlikely your prayers will be fulfilled. Confucius ironically stated, "Do not unto others what you would not want done to you."

Taoism teaches universal duality, the Ying – Yang. Over two thousand years ago, the Chinese philosopher Lao Tzu noted, "For every positive action there is a positive reaction." He also taught, "If a tree does not bend with the wind, it will break." For us, this means we need to open our minds, be receptive to new ideas, and be willing to change for the better!

Henry Ford, the inventor of the automobile, sums up the idea of "belief" most aptly. "We do, in fact, achieve what we believe. This includes survival or success in any of life's ventures. Our only limit is the depth of our beliefs. Our outlook is the greatest influence on that belief. If we do not believe it can be achieved, we will not achieve it unless we can change our attitude."

The material discussed in this chapter will help you develop a positive belief system. By developing positive attitudes, we change our thought patterns, we change our belief systems, and we change our lives. When we believe, we accomplish all we set out to do.

Success, survival, happiness, honesty, self-discipline, and good relationships all depend on positive attitudes.

Another key ingredient necessary for success in technical diving, or in life in general is setting goals. This is the process of defining an objective we desire to accomplish. Success is simply the achievement of our goals. To effectively utilize the technique of setting and realizing goals, we must follow a three-step process. First, we must define exactly what we want. Second, steps must be defined to consummate the goal. Third, we must develop a belief in the attainment of the goal.

Goals are achieved one step at a time. When we accomplished one step, we move on to the next. A belief system also develops in the steps we pursue. Once the mind believes in a realistic goal, it can be fulfilled. Steps taken in orderly progression allow the mind to fully believe in success.

It's a smart idea to write down your goals. In business, it's common to set long-term goals. The long-term goal is then broken down into short-term goals, usually annual goals. Accomplishing each intermediate goal brings long-term success closer.

The same process works in diving. This is true whether your goal is to be a good diver or a record-setting explorer. Once written, the subconscious mind begins to program itself. The use of affirmations and the act of visualizing the goal will speed up its occurrence. Once a given goal is attained, new goals should be envisioned.

The ability to focus a talent, which is mainly developed through meditation, can be enhanced by a few simple exercises. One of the best exercises is simply observing a clock's second hand sweep and concentrating on its movement. The key to this exercise is to dismiss all other thoughts that may present themselves during the exercise. This type of control is essential when facing threatening situations. The key is learning to focus and direct the mind in selective fashion.

Survival depends on being capable of rejecting negative thoughts. A diver who masters the ability to focus can overcome nearly all threatening situations. Under duress, negative emotions and thoughts will flow in an unconditioned mind. If these negative thoughts are allowed a mental audience, they lead to worry, which amplifies, stress and can lead to reactions that culminate in death.

Several years ago, an article appeared in a dive

> "A diver who masters the ability to focus can overcome nearly all threatening situations."

happened to them could happen to anyone. Second, our out-of-air diver survived because he kept his head together by fighting stress and panic. He never stopped thinking! He analyzed the situation and he remained focused throughout the ordeal. And, most importantly of all, he didn't stop. He did not quit. He kept on kicking and kicking, and as a result, he's still alive and able to tell the story!

If all the steps and procedures referenced in this chapter are incorporated into your habits, you will achieve any goal you set providing that you develop a positive, realistic belief in these processes. Saying, "I wanna do it" does not accomplish anything. It is kind of like the Janis Joplin song, "Oh Lord, won't you buy me a Mercedes Benz." Want and belief is not the same thing.

Wanting something does not produce it. Belief accomplishes all. You must program your mind to believe. You must THINK and mentally picture the goal continuously. You must train and make whatever sacrifices are needed to realize your goals!

Survival Training

To merely say that survival training is extremely important would be an understatement. In fact, it's necessary if you want to keep on living! Survival training's benefits are summed up in the book *Safe Cave Diving,* written in 1973. Bob Smith, a contributing author, stated in the stress chapter, "When faced with dying or achieving the impossible, some people choose to live."

Survival training enables divers to exemplify Bob's very apt statement. In fact, it teaches you how to focus your mind on the job of staying alive while, at the same time, making wonderful discoveries. And, importantly, it teaches you how to be physically tough and mentally disciplined through a winning attitude.

This training program addresses technical diving risks for both recreational and exploratory divers. It is

"Wanting something does not produce it. Belief accomplishes all. You must program your mind to believe."

publication praising a diver who died. The name of the publication or that of the diver doesn't matter. The article described how the dead diver was found, dive slate in hand. It went on to say that the diver wrote a letter in wonderfully long and articulate prose to his loved ones. A touching story was presented, one of love and concern for those people dear to him. While it's admirable this person devoted the last moments of life to those he loved, it also brought up another thought. In his perceived moment of tragedy, it appears the diver stopped fighting. Perhaps, the diver died because he gave up instead of trying to solve problems. In this case, it is quite possible that if the diver spent the time swimming and thinking - he might be alive today!

Another story that is a good example a disciplined individual's desire to survive is about a cave diver in his late 40's who was diving in a popular North Florida site. He was in extremely good physical condition and worked out every day. On the day of the incident, he was driving with two buddies. The three divers became separated. During the ensuing events, our diver found himself separated and disoriented.

When he finally figured out where he was, 2,000 ft (610 m) back in the cave, he only had 400 psig (27 bar) in his primaries and he was 200 ft (61 m) away from his stage bottle. When he was 100 ft (30 m) from his stage bottle, his air ran out. Through sheer willpower and a desire to survive, our diver swam the last 100 ft (30 m) with only the air in his lungs.

There are two points to this story. First, by all accounts, the dive team followed all the rules. What essential to make informed decisions. A problem 2,000 feet (610 m) into an overhead environment is far more difficult to manage than a problem in open water. By reviewing the accidents in diving, it is apparent that technical diving does have risk. We must be aware of the risks and know how to evaluate them.

Several years prior to his death, Sheck Exley introduced the merits of breaking down accidents into steps and analyzing the mechanisms that produced the incident. The majority of accidents result from a diver's mistakes. In other words, your life may depend on your ability to think fast and to get it right the first time. If you're tired or hurt, a buddy may be able to help you swim for a little while and, if necessary, share gas. However, you're the only one that can really control your breathing rate, and you're also the only one who knows when your "you know what" is in sling. Ultimately only you can save it!

To react favorably in the face of a physical threat, precondition yourself to as many uncomfortable yet life-dependent variables as possible. A good example is your ability to survive in the event of a real gas-sharing emergency. In a real emergency, your buddy is going to be more than an arm's length away. Your buddy is probably swimming and not looking directly at you.

In your mind, visualize this scenario: you're 60 ft (18 m) down. Everything beyond your beam of light is pitch-black. Worse still, you're 1,000 ft (305 m) from the up-line and you've had a total gas supply failure. Perhaps your regulator has broken. Picture yourself not panicking. All you have to do is just swim nonchalantly over to your buddy and tap on their shoulder to get their attention. They signal, "What is wrong?" You casually indicate, "I am out of air. Notice how blue my face is?" They acknowledge that you've looked better. You go onto inquire ever so meekly, "Would you please let me share

Tom Mount uses resistance and weight training to increase his survivability. Photo by Patti Mount.

your air?" They say, "Sure, no problem!"

Gas sharing rarely goes as smoothly as the above scenario. In fact, gas sharing requires precision teamwork. All team members involved must know their roles and be able to execute them without making mistakes. The life of the out-of-air diver is at stake, and probably those of the team members as well. After all, it's their air that's being shared.

The best way to ensure that buddy breathing never becomes a nightmare is through the regular practice of out-of-air drills that stimulate the stress of a "real" situation. Prior to implementing gas sharing and breath holding survival skills, begin by swimming a set distance underwater without breathing. If this is hard, remind yourself of the importance of being able to cope with the feeling of needing to breathe.

Keep in mind that in real situation, your buddy will be swimming. You will have to get their attention and/or overtake them in order to find an air source. In these drills, the actual breath holding duration rarely exceeds 35-45 seconds. There is no real danger of blackout and no true physiological demand for air. There is a psychological scream as the mind and body exceed the time at which it is conditioned to breathe. This skill is paramount for divers who may be exposed to real out-of-air situations. It is not, and is not approached as, a fitness test or "toughness skill."

The gas sharing exercise involves swimming without air 60-75 ft (18-23 m) to a buddy, gaining their attention and initiating gas sharing. Both divers will then remain at rest for at least three breaths to allow the out-of-air diver to regain respiratory control. Both divers then perform a timed swim. The timed swim is not for speed. The divers must maintain a normal swim pace. If the divers swim too fast, additional stress is developed and gas consumption is increased. This, of course, may inhibit them from making it to the surface. On the other hand, if the pace is too slow, they may not have enough gas to reach the surface. The key is that the timed swim be based on a normal swim pace.

Now, let's analyze why this skill helps divers develop survival instincts. If faced with a "real" out of air situation, the subconscious mind "knows" it can deal with it. The mind has been preconditioned to handle the emergency. It means that the diver knows how it feels to need and really want air without being forced to "turn blue". It means being disciplined and in control when faced with adverse conditions.

Additional training skills include the performance of other life support and equipment familiarity skills. A few essentials include: gas shutdowns, use of safety lines, lost diver procedures, and navigating a line in blackout conditions (simulated by closing the eyes). Training and certification, if done properly, prepare divers for the stress that coincides with in-water emergencies.

The Importance of Fitness

The ideal technical diver is a finely tuned individual, both mentally and physically. Good physical fitness allows the diver to handle his equipment without staggering under its weight. It permits him/her to swim long distances without tiring. Even the diver who uses a diver propulsion vehicle (DPV) must be physically fit. This diver is at special risk if the DPV malfunction during the course of a dive and they are unfit to handle the situation.

Out-of-shape divers are prone to cramps, unable to control respiration and incapable of providing physical assistance in an emergency. Their work and resting RMV is dramatically different. Fit divers tend to develop coordination as part of their training. This enables them to become more skillful diving technicians. Mental fitness is a must for maintaining self-discipline. Much of the training in a technical program is aimed at developing mental control.

It is appropriate to say that physically unfit divers should avoid technical diving. The non-thinking diver is not qualified for technical diving. Serious deficiencies in either mental or physical fitness place a diver at much greater risk in the diving environment.

A diver needs to be physically fit to prevent injury. Cardiovascular fitness provides the stamina to be comfortable while swimming extended distances in SCUBA gear. It has been documented that unfit divers may retain up to 50%

Fit divers are safer divers. Photo by Eric Frehsee.

more CO_2 than physically fit divers. This is important. CO_2 is additive to early fatigue, decompression illness, and inert gas narcosis and oxygen toxicity. In other words, excess CO_2 may hurt you. Increased CO_2 may also lead to uncontrolled respiration. It is a major factor in loss of consciousness and drowning.

The first step on the road to survival training involves getting a complete physical at your doctor's office. The second step is beginning a physical conditioning program. The initial training should incorporate some exercise for muscular toning and a graduated level of cardiovascular conditioning. In selecting the muscular toning exercise, resistance with weights or machinery is effective. This part of the regime should simulate actions using muscles that you will need for your style of diving. (For example, high pull-ups will simulate the act of lifting tanks.)

Resistance training needs to be balanced. Extending and contracting muscles prevents an imbalance by working both groups of muscles. Unbalanced musculature may lead to injury. Special attention should be placed on stomach and lower back muscles. These muscles are subjected to strain in technical diving environments. This is especially true when managing equipment.

This two-step approach to fitness is the first level of survival training. The survival benefit is developing the discipline to enter and maintain a fitness program. Even the most devout athletes require discipline. There are days when excuses abound to avoid a training session. There will be days when you literally drag yourself into a workout. Getting the job done means you are developing a good survival instinct. It is on these days you are going beyond your comfort zone. The days you give in and do not workout can be viewed as diminished survival days.

Once the first two basic steps have been initiated and a reasonable degree of fitness has evolved, it's time to begin the third step. Hard-core survival training takes all you can muster mentally and physically. This is an

> ## "The first step on the road to survival training involves getting a complete physical at your doctor's office."

ongoing, increasingly tough and demanding pace. The benefits will greatly enhance your ability to overcome adversity and survive. In this training, we select a given exercise and assign three goals. The first goal is a time factor. The second is distance or performance measurement. The third separates us from the pack. We will accomplish these goals at all cost! Keep in mind this is a gradual process. Training becomes addictive once current goals become less challenging. Mentally these must be viewed as life or death achievements.

Survival abilities can be developed, enhanced and maintained on land more conveniently and effectively than underwater. The programs to develop survival conditioning go beyond cardiovascular training. Many physical trainers and physiologist define cardiovascular-level training as the point where an elevated pulse is maintained for at least 20 minutes. During this period, the individual should be able to carry on a conversation without interrupting the exercise pace.

However, when performing survival training, exercise should be well beyond the conversation level. When you've reached this plateau, the only voice you'll be able to muster is the one in your mind that says, "Don't quit. Keep going!" This is unquestionably a maximum level performance. The entire program is aimed at functioning beyond your comfort level and maintaining that level. The parameters involve maintaining maximum, sustained effort while keeping a constant respiratory rate. This requires discipline to allow increased volume without a corresponding increase in respiratory rate. Obviously, it takes more than a few training sessions to master.

Controlling your respiratory rate under stress, means overcoming interfering messages generated by the autonomic nervous system. Efficient respiration is vital for developing good discipline when using SCUBA gear. As divers, we deal with an assortment of variables requiring us to maintain a slow inhalation and exhalation rate. A few of these variables include a regulator's breathing resistance, drag, and the density produced by the depth and/or gas mixture. By controlling our respiratory rates, we have taken the first step in mental control. In this instance, limited control of the ANS has been gained.

A stair climber or step machine is an excellent survival-training tool. I personally use and recommend it. Establish a maximum comfortable level that you can maintain. Next, gradually boost the level until you are exercising a minimum of 40 minutes.

As your fitness improves, incorporate interval training. After two minutes on the climber, raise the difficulty by one level. Maintain this level for two

Martial arts students practicing energy building exercises. Photo by Tom Mount.

minutes. Resume the previous level and repeat this cycle every two minutes. Throughout this routine, maintain a constant and slow respiratory rate. A good initial respiratory rate is achieved by inhaling approximately six seconds, and pausing no more than three seconds in between breaths. Finally, exhale for six seconds.

Once you've mastered the initial step in interval training, increase your level to the maximum that can be maintained for 20 minutes. Next, reduce the level by one and complete five additional minutes. Start increasing the intensity of interval training. After three minutes, return to the next higher level for another three minutes. Finally, repeat this procedure for 30 minutes and raise the "bump up" intervals to five minutes each.

This maximum exercise should be maintained throughout the session. Gradually increase the total time from 20-40 minutes. When you've reached the upper level and can maintain it, it's time to begin survival training.

Survival training exceeds the limits of normal interval training. It means your workout session is a maximum effort from beginning to end. I do the following. On my stair climber I set the upper level at 12. This translates to 20.3 flights of stair-per-minute. I do the entire 40 minutes at this level. My performance goal is 40 minutes and 820 floors, or an average of 20.5 floors-per-minute. The acceptable range is from 770 floors to 820 floors.

When I maintain this level, my survivability is rated as certain. When I climb less than 770 floors, I score myself with reduced survival abilities. As long as I complete the time and remain between 725 and 750 floors, a good survivability exists. If less than 725 but more than 675 floors are completed, the survivability is average. When the total floors climbed are between 650 and 675, survivability is low. With less than 650 floors, the rating is poor. When I'm unable to complete the exercises, I rate my odds for survival at zero. In my training philosophy, I "die" on those days.

During these drills, try to complete all of your goals. Even on those days when you cannot maintain the accelerated rates, at least complete the time objective. Occasionally, it will be necessary for you to actually stop (just as in a stressful diving situation), regain respiratory and/or mental control, and resume exercising. Going the full time limit is paramount. Quitting too soon means you probably won't survive. Every one of us has read about divers who quit trying. When they quit trying, they died!

The level of intensity in survival training varies from person to person. Everyone should be able to discover a personal system and rating code. The tougher you train, the greater your survivability factor is. Jim Lockwood, for example, has survived near impossible situations. His workouts on the stair climber last over 1-½ hours. He goes "flat out." He also finds time for a 70-100 mile (112-161 km) bicycle ride 2–3 times a week. In season, he combines swimming and kayaking with the same intensity of training.

"Quitting too soon means you probably won't survive."

Experiment with a level of exercise that will force you to become more mentally and physically disciplined. This combination of mental and physical self-control is paramount to your survival. While training, your body and mind will often cry out for relief. When this happens, visualize yourself in a critical situation. Your only hope of survival is to keep going. When you want to stop and rest, dig deep within yourself and produce that extra burst of mental power to drive your physical body to success. On those really tough days, give yourself a reward for completing a survival session. Getting the job done when it's the hardest improves your survivability factor. On the easy days, and they are few, you simply maintain and reconfirm your abilities.

Cross training is an excellent to help increase fitness and prevent boredom. Swimming, especially with fins, is an excellent way to improve stamina and endurance. Set up your program for maximum effort. This may sound extreme. It is. However, it also conditions both your body and mind for a better survival level. I know this to be true from dozens of personal experiences,

including a plane crash.

Both Patti Mount and I survived a plane crash with multiple injuries. We were in the water fighting for our lives for over 3 ½ hours. Patti was semi-conscious and unconsciousness for much of this time. The entire 3 ½ hours was spent swimming, as our emergency life-raft sank faster than our plane. The only flotation device I could think of involved using my blue jeans, which I made into a float for Patti. Thanks to our survival training, we are both alive today.

The importance of physical fitness should be evident by this time, but as it relates to both mental and physical discipline, we will take a more in-depth look at the benefits of fitness for technical divers.

Summary

By incorporating the survival training I have described, a positive belief system evolves. Inner awareness is created. We become in tune with our "intuitive selves" and our physical and mental abilities. We accomplish what our belief system dictates. People achieve beliefs, not undirected daydreams. However, through some of the above practices, it is possible to turn daydreams into beliefs systems.

When asked what the *tech* in the phrase *tech diver* stands for, most would answer: technical. True, but by the same token, tech could - and should - refer to technique. Proper underwater posture and swimming technique are probably the most overlooked yet critical ingredients of safe and enjoyable diving. This includes a variety of frog kicks, modified flutter kicks, and one-legged kicks. You will also practice "fin sculling" and heel-toe kicks. Your instructor will demonstrate the fining techniques described in this manual.

Kicking Techniques

Technical diving involves precision swimming. You will also be required to swim longer distances than in most open water dives. These kicks will provide the necessary precision, and help you with your endurance: Frog kicks consist of the cave frog kick, a modified frog kick, and the power frog kick. The most common of these is the cave frog kick.

A cave frog kick is performed with your body in a horizontal posture. First, the fins slide gracefully - without power - outward to a full extension. In most cases, the legs will remain slightly elevated to maintain maximum distance from the cave floor. The fins are then cupped by twisting the ankles and the power stroke is on the inward travel portion of the kick. It will place demands on your leg muscles as you deliver the kick in powerful,

continuous strokes.

The modified frog kick is identical except the range of the kick is shortened. Occasionally this kick will utilize only a range of motion created from the movement of the ankle, i.e. a parallel, horizontal "flutter." A diver using this kick may travel less than a foot in some circumstances.

The power frog kick is another variation. Both the extension and retraction portions of the kick are executed with more power.

Modified flutter kicks are the most common of technical propulsion skills. Such kicks involve an up-and down (vertical scissors) leg motion and are executed while swimming horizontally with your body parallel to the bottom. When using this kick, make sure your downward thrust does not extend below your body axis. To execute a modified flutter kick, a diver extends his legs and uses a vertical scissors motion to propel himself forward. To avoid silting, the sweep should not extend lower than the horizontal axis.

Shuffle kicks are another variation of the flutter kick that is most often used in areas where potential silting is a major concern. This kick involves a carefully controlled vertical scissors motion. The kick begins above the diver's back and only travels a distance of one-quarter to one-half of the distance to the diver's horizontal axis. The one-legged shuffle kick was developed for use when leg cramps occur. It also

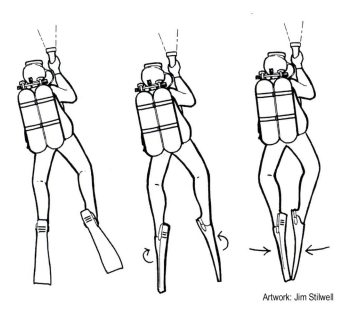

Artwork: Jim Stilwell

Artwork: Jim Stilwell

works well in silt. This kick uses a full range of motion similar to the modified flutter. The difference is that one leg is a kicking leg and the other a resting leg. The kicking leg travels downward until it rests on the diver's other leg, which is extended but not moved. The extended leg serves as a shield to minimize fin turbulence on the down stroke.

Heel toe, or ankle kicks are a very controlled flutter kick. Both legs are extended and the kick is delivered by flexing your ankles up and down. This motion effectively

Artwork: Jim Stilwell

controls silting, provided the diver executes the kick with accuracy and does not extend the kick to exaggerated distances below the horizontal axis.

Using Your Hands

When swimming with fins, a diver's hands are normally kept close to the body. Technical divers should learn to not wave their hands in an attempt to maintain placement or balance. The turbulence caused by this type of reactionary hand sculling may result in substantial silting. Gentle, deliberate sculling, on the other hand, is a tool that is useful to slightly reposition the diver.

"Pull and glide" is a technique developed by cave divers to pull themselves along a wall with hand and arm motions. This technique is also usable in wrecks and in open water current dives where there is appropriate structure to grasp.

Just as it sounds, this technique uses a diver's hands to grasp a structure and pull their body forward. A glide is often added when there is mild or no current, or a following current. Pull by "clamping" with the palm of your hand and your fingers – not fingertips. If you persist in using your fingertips to propel yourself, you'll remove most of your fingerprints!

"Finger walking" is a technique used when sandy floors, bottoms or decks are encountered. Keep your feet high to avoid kicking up the bottom. Aside from communicating and manipulating your equipment, your

fingers maintain line contact in overhead environments. This is only done when visibility requires you to touch the line.

Locating Other Divers

When divers explore overhead environments or engage in open water night dives, keeping track of dive buddies can become a challenge. Remember, the only light available is that which your dive team creates. As long as the "light distance" between team members remains constant, the pace is probably okay. If you notice a buddy's light dimming, this usually indicates the pace should be slowed. To get a buddy's attention, the customary practice is to sweep your light in a circular motion on the bottom or wall of an overhead environment (not in your buddy's eyes) or along the bottom in open water.

The best way to locate a dive buddy swimming behind you is to dip your head down and look between your legs. This is much more efficient than stopping and turning around. Sometimes this is the only way to locate your buddy.

When diving at night or in overhead environments, buddy checks must involve all dive team members. OKs are communicated from every diver. Start with the last diver passing the OK verification forward to the lead diver. As soon as a problem arises, the diver advised of the problem sweeps his light in a vertical motion to the diver in front of him. The signal is passed forward until the lead diver is advised and the team stops.

> "The best way to locate a dive buddy swimming behind you is to dip your head down and look between your legs."

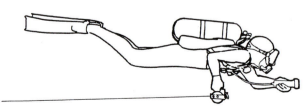

Technical diver demonstrating correct swim posture

Artwork: Jim Stilwell

Stage Diving

Stage diving, or using additional cylinders to increase swim time or bottom time, requires considerable thought and planning. Staging allows the diver to extend the distance of safe exploration, but due to being further away from the return point of the dive may also produce additional time pressure stress. Training and a gradual increase in penetration distances and bottom times will help offset this stress.

Stage diving is similar to flying an airplane. The diver must think well ahead of his/her position. By thinking ahead and being familiar with stage techniques, the diver avoids delays during stage drops and retrievals, and will avoid sudden changes in buoyancy. Your instructor will introduce you to stage diving techniques as applicable to either decompression stage management or penetration staging.

Two cave divers in a Mexican Cenote Photo by Steve Gerrard.

Diver Propulsion Vehicles (DPV)

Using a diver propulsion vehicle (DPV) is the closest thing to space travel one can imagine. A DPV diver must think in terms of minutes ahead of his present position. Prior to enrolling in the IANTD DPV course, you must become proficient in all the relevant skills of the technical diver and should be completely comfortable with stage diving, long swim distances, orientation and the ability to read the environment.

Once DPV diving becomes a part of your repertoire, it would be prudent to periodically make long swim dives to keep track of the amount of gas used per distance traveled when swimming as opposed to riding the DPV. With modern DPVs, it is possible to attain penetration distances that the diver could not return from in the event of a DPV failure. Constant physical training and periodic long stage dives will provide an understanding of your swim limits and assist in the development of the proper disciplines needed to cope with DPV emergencies.

Summary

It is very important that you learn all of the techniques discussed in this chapter. It takes practice and experience to develop the combinations of techniques that yield the best performance with a minimum of effort. Good technique, maintaining an acceptable level of physical conditioning, developing mind control and ongoing practice will result in lower gas consumption, less drag, increased forward momentum, less fatigue and generally more enjoyable diving.

Notes:

Photo by Stephen Frink

Photo Courtesy of Carl Bayer

Photo by Andrew Goldby

Photo Courtesy of Rudi Asseer

Photo by Jim Kozmik

Photo by Chris Man

Photo by Tom Mount

Photo by Stefan Besier

Photo by Tom Mount

Photo Courtesy of OMG

Photo Courtesy of Dive Rite

Glossary of Terms

Air Cell: Another term for a buoyancy compensator (**BC**). See **BC**.

ABS: A type of high impact plastic. **Abs,** slang for abdominal muscles or it also refers to 'absolute.'

ADP: Adenosine Diphosphate, see **Adenosine Triphosphate** above.

ATA: Atmospheres Absolute. May be used interchangeably with the term 'Bar' when referring to Partial Pressures.

ATM: Atmospheres, Imperial-US measurement of pressure equal to 14.7 **psi.**

Bar: Metric measurement of pressure approximately equal to 1 atmosphere (**atm**) or 14.7 psi. May be used interchangeably with the term 'ATA' when referring to Partial Pressures.

BC or BCD: Buoyancy Compensating Device. A device used to either adjust a divers buoyancy or provide surface floatation. **BC**'s are not considered Personal Floatation Devices (PFD's) which are required equipment by certain state and federal agencies under certain circumstances.

BT: Bottom Time.

C: Centigrade, see **Centigrade/Celsius.**

Carbon Dioxide: See **CO_2**.

Carbon Monoxide: See **CO**.

Cardiac: Having to do with the heart.

cc: Cubic Centimeters.

Centigrade/Celsius: Metric measurement of temperature. To convert

Centigrade/Celsius to Fahrenheit, multiply by 9/5 (1.80) and add 32.

CFM: Cubic Feet per **Minute,** Imperial-US measurement of volume flow.

cm: Centimeter, metric length measure. 1 inch equals 2.54 centimeters.

CNS: Central Nervous System.

CNS% or %CNS: The percent of central nervous system oxygen exposure.

CO: Carbon monoxide, a highly toxic, colorless, odorless, and tasteless gas produced by the combustion of hydrocarbons (petroleum fuels used in engines, and smoking tobacco or cannabis.)

CO_2: Carbon dioxide. A normal by-product of **respiration,** Carbon dioxide can be harmful if allowed to accumulate. See **Hypercapnia.**

CO_2 Retention: The build up of carbon dioxide in body tissue. Individuals that tend to accumulate carbon dioxide more than average are termed **CO_2 retainers.**

CON-VENTID: Mnemonic for the symptoms of oxygen poisoning.

Cubic Feet: Imperial-US measurement of volume. Another way of expressing this volume is **feet cubed** or **Ft^3**.

Cu. Ft.: Cubic Feet, see cubic feet.

DAN: Divers Alert Network.

D-ring: A 'd' shaped ring used for attaching equipment.

DCI: Decompression illness/injury, the direct result of not allowing for the safe elimination of excess or accumulated gas in body tissue. Also referred to as **DCS,** decompression sickness. Although there are subtle differences in medical terminology for decompression illness, decompression injury, and decompression sickness, the end result is the same - treatment in a very expensive recompression chamber.

DCS: Decompression Sickness. See **DCI**.

Deco: Slang for the word 'decompression', i.e., deco bottle or deco stop.

DIN: Deutsches Institut für Normung, a European regulatory association.

Doppler Effect or **Doppler Studies:** An acoustic measuring device or method used by scientists to measure the passage of bubbles in the arteries or veins of divers. A Doppler device for divers would be, in essence, a bubble counter.

Doubles: Two **SCUBA** cylinders joined together by a manifold to create a <u>single</u> gas supply. (In effect, 'doubling' the available gas supply.) Although some use the terms **twins** and **doubles** almost interchangeably, there is a very critical, life or death, difference between the two concepts. See also **twins** which is a different and very dangerous concept. See also **side mount**.

DPV: Diver Propulsion Vehicle, alias scooter, sled, torpedo, etc.; Any motorized device used for transporting submerged divers.

EAD: Equivalent Air Depth.

EAR: European term for Rescue Breathing.

EAN: Enriched Air **Nitrox.**

EANx: Abbreviation used to describe a generic **Nitrox** blend. A 36% oxygen **Nitrox** blend is EAN 36.

EDU: United States Navy Experimental Diving Unit.

END: Equivalent Nitrogen Depth.

Enzyme: A highly specialized, biologically active protein. **Enzymes** are the tools with which the body controls **metabolism.**

EPIRB: Emergency Positioning Indicator Radio Beacon that is compact and self contained.

EST: Electroshock Therapy.

Fahrenheit: Imperial-US measurement of temperature. To convert **Fahrenheit** to **Centigrade/Celsius,** subtract 32 and multiply by 5/9 (.556).

Feet: Imperial-US measurement of length or depth. 1 **foot** equals .305 **meters.**

Feet cubed: Imperial-US measurement of volume. 1 **cubic foot** equals 28.32 **free liters.**

FFW: Feet fresh water. Imperial-US measurement of depth in feet of fresh water. Very rarely used.

Fg: Fraction (percentage) of a gas in a mix.

FLPM: Free Liters Per Minute.

FN_2: Fraction of Nitrogen.

FO_2: Fraction of **Oxygen** in a mix.

Free Radical: A highly destructive, 'hot' molecule of usually some oxygen compound. **Free radicals** are short lived because they are so energetically active (looking for something to bind to or combine with). They can and will bind to just about any other molecule either destroying that molecule or disrupting its function.

FSW: Feet Salt Water. Imperial-US measurement of depth in feet of salt water.

Ft: Feet, see **feet**.

Ft^3: Cubic Feet, see **feet cubed**.

GABA: Gamma-aminobutyric Acid. **GABA** is a neurotransmitter responsible for brain functioning.

g/l: Grams per **liter**.

HBO: Hyperbaric Oxygen or Hyperbaric Oxygenation.

He: See **helium.**

Heliair: Any mixture of air and helium.

Heliox: Any mixture of oxygen and helium.

Helium: An inert biologically unreactive gas.

Hgb: Abbreviation for **Hemoglobin**.

Hogarth or **Hogarthian Style:** A particular gear configuration, some say gear configuration philosophy, named in honor of William Hogarth Main.

HSE: Health and Safety Executive, United Kingdom.

Hypercapnia: A potentially fatal condition for divers caused by an excessive build up of **carbon dioxide** in either body tissue or inspired air.

IANTD: The International Association of Nitrox and Technical Divers.

No J entries

Kit: European term referring to the dive gear or equipment needed for a dive. Somewhat analogous to the American terms 'rig' or 'gear'.

Kiting or kiting up: European terms referring to the act of outfitting or dressing for a dive. Analogous to the American term 'suiting up' or 'gearing up'.

kPa: KiloPascals. Metric measurement of pressure. See also **mmHg**.

L: Liter, see **liter**.

Liter: Metric measurement for volume. 1 **liter** equals 0.035 **cubic feet**. One of the finer points of the metric system is that a **liter** of gas is referred to differently from a **liter** of a liquid. **Liters** of gas are formally referred to as **free liters**. Off the record, unless one is a chemist, a **liter** of gas is basically the same as a **free liter** of gas. Many of our international colleagues, especially British colleagues, request that IANTD use the 'proper' terminology to refer to a **liter** of gas as being a **free liter** of gas.

m: Meter, see **meter**.

mbar: Millibar.

Meds: Medications.

Meter: Metric measurement of length or depth. 1 **meter** equals 3.28 **feet**.

MFW: Meter Fresh Water. Metric measurement of depth in meters of fresh water.

ml: Milliliter. Metric measurement of volume.

mm: Millimeter. Metric measurement of length.

mmHg: Millimeters of mercury. Imperial-US measurement for pressure.

MOD: Maximum Operational Depth.

"Mr. Murphy": American slang name for a fictional character. See **Murphy's Law**.

MSW: Meters Salt Water. Metric measurement of depth in meters of salt water.

Murphy's Law: Anything that can go wrong will go wrong.

 NOAA: The National Oceanic and Atmospheric Administration (United States).

Narcosis: A detrimental physiological and mental state produced by high levels of absorbed nitrogen (**nitrogen narcosis**) or inert gases (**inert gas narcosis**) such as Hydrogen or Neon

Ne: Neon, an inert biologically unreactive gas.

Nitrogen: An 'inert' diatomic (2 atom) gas. Air consists of approximately 78% diatomic nitrogen. Actually, diatomic nitrogen is chemically unreactive (not inert) in higher life forms because the two molecules are so tightly bound together. Lower life forms, such as nitrogen-fixing bacterial, can use (metabolize) diatomic nitrogen.

Nitrogen narcosis: See **narcosis**.

Nitrox: Any gas mixture of oxygen and nitrogen other than air (Air being approximately 21% oxygen).

NREM: Non-Rapid Eye Movement. See **REM**.

NSAIDS: Non-steroidal anti-inflammatory drugs.

 O_2: The chemical representation for diatomic **oxygen**. See **oxygen**.

OMS: Ocean Management Systems. A manufacturer of technical diving equipment. Other manufacturers that specifically cater to technical diving include DiveRite, Zeagle, etc.

OTC: Over The Counter.

OTU: Oxygen Toxicity Unit.
Oxygen: Required to sustain life (ie., run **metabolism**), **oxygen** is nature's most common oxidant and is a necessary ingredient required for combustion/**respiration**.

 P: Usually refers to 'pressure.'

Pg: Partial pressure of a gas.

pH: A measurement of the hydrogen ion concentration in solution (such as blood).

PO_2: Partial pressure of **oxygen**.

PPO_2: Same as **PO_2**.

PSI: Pounds per Square Inch. Imperial-US measurement for pressure.

PSIG: Pounds per Square Inch Gauge. Imperial-US measurement for gauge pressure (for absolute pressure, add 14.7 pound per square inch to PSIG)

Pulmonary: Having to do with the lungs.

 RBC: Red Blood Cell.

Respiration: A metabolic process that involves the exchange of gases. In air breathing mammals (most divers would qualify), Inhaled **oxygen** (an oxidizer), is exchanged with exhaled **Carbon Dioxide** (a waste by-product of metabolism).

RMV: Respiratory Minute Volume.

RNT: Residual Nitrogen Time.

RNPL: Royal Naval Physiologic Laboratory.

Rule of Thirds: A simple gas management technique specifying that divers use only one third of their available gas supply for 'penetration' (or descent into a dive). Upon expending the first third of air, the diver exits (ascends) using the second third of air. Upon reaching the exit point, the diver should have the full measure of the last third of their gas supply remaining.

S **S-Drill:** 'Safety' drill performed before all technical dives.

SAC: Surface Air Consumption.

SCUBA: Self Contained Underwater Breathing Apparatus.

SDO: Surface Decompression using Oxygen.

Side Mount: Term used to describe a rig that enables a diver to wear two

SCUBA cylinders, one cylinder on each side of the diver. Unlike **twins** that are also independent, **side mounted** cylinders allow the diver to directly

inspect and manage the two independent systems. Note: Some sources occasionally refer to stages as **side mount**.

SIT: Surface Interval Time.

SPG: Submersible Pressure Gauge.

SRF: Surface Ratio Factor.

Sur-D: Surface Decompression.

 TOD: Target Operating Depth.

 Trimix: Any breathable mixture of **Nitrogen, Oxygen,** and **Helium.**

Twins: Term used in the United States to describe a rig where two independent **SCUBA** cylinders are worn on the back creating 'twin' independent air supplies. [British sources - such as author Kevin Gurr - often refer to **doubles** (see **doubles**) as 'twins'.] Back-mounted dual independent gas supplies (what divers refer to in the United States as **twins**) have been shown to be a major cause of diving fatalities.

 UHMS: The Undersea and Hyperbaric Medicine Society.

 V_E: Is actually pronounced "V dot E" and refers to expired total ventilation.

VO_2: A measure of a divers ability to utilize oxygen.

VPA: Sodium Valproate, enhances **GABA**, see chapter 11.

 WBC: White Blood Cells.

X No X entries.

Y No Y entries.

Z No Z entries.

For a more extensive glossary, please consult the IANTD Technical Diver Encyclopedia, *which is an excellent reference book and a recommended companion to the Tek Lite diver course and manual. Ask your instructor for more information.*